# NLP &

## RELATIONSHIPS

ROBIN PRIOR & JOSEPH O'CONNOR

*Simple strategies to make*

*your relationships work*

Element
An Imprint of HarperCollins*Publishers*
77–85 Fulham Palace Road
Hammersmith, London W6 8JB

The website address is: www.thorsonselement.com

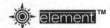 ™

and *Element* are trademarks of
HarperCollins*Publishers* Limited

Published by Thorsons, an imprint of HarperCollins*Publishers* 2000
This edtion published by Element 2002

10

A catalogue record for this book
is available from the British Library

ISBN-13  978-0-7225-3868-5
ISBN-10  0-7225-3868-5

Printed and bound in Great Britain by
Clays Ltd, St Ives plc

This book is proudly printed on paper which contains wood
from well-managed forests, certified in accordance with
the rules of the Forest Stewardship Council.
For more information about FSC,
please visit www.fsc.org

**Mixed Sources**
Product group from well-managed
forests and other controlled sources
www.fsc.org  Cert no. SW-COC-1806
© 1996 Forest Stewardship Council

# Contents

To Debbie and Jill

# Preface

■ 'Relationship' – a simple word and one that hides some of the richest, most complex and meaningful questions. Relationships make us human, they hold our world together. The happiness and quality of our lives depend on them. They make us who we are: our relationships with our parents, our teachers, friends, family and lovers. Also, throughout our life we each have a changing relationship with ourselves. That relationship makes it easy or hard to be alone.

Although life can be fulfilling on your own or in a poor relationship, for most people a relationship that works is the foundation stone upon which the rest of their lives is built. To many, love, partnership, trust, companionship and intimacy are as vital to them as water and air. Fulfilling relationships are not the preserve of the rich, famous, talented or privileged. Neither do these advantages make it any easier to have good relationships (sometimes quite the opposite). We can all form partnerships that bring pleasure and satisfaction.

There have been more books on the making and breaking of intimate relationships than perhaps any other subject. Everyone has had these experiences. Everyone is interested. Everyone wants to know how to have more satisfying and fulfilling relationships. The bad news is that the answer is not to be found in a book. The good news is the power is within yourself. This book explores the ways in which you can use that power. It explores intimate relationships with sexual partners and close friends, those relationships that give you the greatest joy when they are good and the worst misery when they are not.

Is there anything new to say about relationships? Yes, there is a great deal. All relationships are different. We all live in the same world, yet we all experience it differently. We all create our own unique subjective world from our experience. One person can be popular, have many friends and have no trouble in attracting sexual partners. Another may be shy, unpopular, have only a few close friends and few sexual partners. We see this every day and while physical attractiveness plays a part, it is only a small part. There is more to it than that.

It takes two to make a relationship. There has to be a give and take. Sometimes we think that if only the other person would change then everything would be fine. When that happens you can almost guarantee that the other person is thinking *exactly* the same thing about you, because a relationship is a dance, not a solitary walk. It is harmony, not two people playing a solo at the same time. What you *can* do is take responsibility for your own part. You can be sure if you change what you are doing significantly, then the other person will not be able to respond in the same way as before.

This book is not, however, about how to change or manipulate others into being what you want them to be. Nor is it about trying to fit into other people's expectations regardless of your own point of view. It is about being more yourself, putting more of yourself into a relationship and letting the other person be themselves too. For this to happen, there has to be a certain level of safety and trust. Building a strong relationship means testing that the foundations are safe. The more of yourself that you bring to a relationship, the greater the possible happiness and fulfilment for both of you. But first you must take responsibility for what you do – it is the least you can do and all you can do.

In looking at how to achieve this, we examine the tension between three parts of ourselves which we experience in relationships. First there is our instinctive nature. That is part of our biological nature. It is the oldest part of ourselves and one we often have to bury deeply in order to live in society. Then there is our social self with all its restraints. Finally, there is our intellectual self – the voice of reason. Put these 'voices' together and we often experience a cacophony. We feel pulled in different directions – there is a fight between what we want at a basic sexual level, the norms and controls of society and our upbringing, and the cool voice that appraises the consequences. We hope this book will help these voices sing in harmony, joining together with our spiritual and emotional experience.

This is not a book on therapy or on putting together fractured relationships, but one about understanding the relationships you have and making them more satisfying. While the proposals are well founded on theory and research, this is also a practical book. It offers many exercises which you can use to explore your relationships.

Relationships are not an easy subject to write about and although this is our second book as co-authors, it brings up some issues for the first time. As usual we want to share our views equally. And having read many books on relationships for our research we believe it is important to get close to you, the reader. We have to have a relationship with you if you are to enjoy this book and get what you want out of it. Some of the books we read left us feeling that the author was somewhat distant. Relationships cannot be viewed completely objectively, like a museum specimen in a glass case. We live and breathe and laugh and cry our relationships. So, how could we make our book personal and warm? We decided to write directly, to share our own experience of relationships. We decided to do this by describing our stories from the first person, marked to show which of us is telling the story. If we are to bare our souls, we want to make sure everyone is clear whose soul is being bared! We also decided that it would be best to concentrate on one person's experience to give a better sense of continuity. Robin won that privilege, so you will find Robin's experience in most of the examples. The non-personal anecdotes are a result of our joint experience.

Now, let's deal with two possible problems. First, the extreme postmodern claim that in order to understand something you have to live it. So can two middle-aged, heterosexual, happily married males know anything worthwhile about the many possible relationship difficulties? To this we would reply, yes, as much as anyone else. If we all had to live everything personally, great fiction in books and plays and films would be impossible. We do not need to experience putting a hand in a fire to know to avoid it. We have seen what happens to others who have done so and there is plenty of information available about the consequences. We all have our experience, and our imagination, and one of the greatest powers of the human imagination is the ability to put ourselves in another person's shoes. Whether you call it empathy or fellow feeling, it is a basic part of being able to build relationships. We are all human and therefore nothing human is alien to us. All books are both limited and enlightened by the author's knowledge and experience. We believe we bring a broad wealth of experience on relationships to this book.

The second question derives from the first. How far can anyone generalize about relationships when we are all so different? Generalizations give directions and starting-points, however your own experience is always true. Generalizations always have exceptions, however they help to clarify the subject either by endorsing your own experience or by allowing you to understand it more clearly by contrast.

Inevitably, our beliefs on this rich and controversial subject affect the way we have written the book. If you disagree with us, that is fine; we are not claiming infallibility.

Building good relationships is a journey. The word itself is static but the reality changes all the time. There is never a point where you can sit back and think, 'Right. That's it. I've done it, I'm in a successful relationship.' The moment you do, we propose, is the moment your relationship is starting to deteriorate. Relationships are created moment to moment by what you are doing right now. We hope this book can show you how you can create ones full of joy and fulfilment.

*Robin Prior*
*Joseph O'Connor*
*June 1999*

# Acknowledgements

For their work with NLP we would like to thank John Grinder and Richard Bandler, the originators, and Robert Dilts, who has added so much. We would also like to acknowledge the following for their work in the fields of human behaviour and relationships: Charles Darwin, Eric Berne, Richard Dawkins, Desmond Morris, Sue Quillian, Dr Janet Reibstein, Marton Tysoe, Dr Clive Bronhall, Anne and Bill Moir, David Jessel, John Gray, Robin Norwood and Cathy Troupp. For their advice and expertise we would also like to thank Fran Reader, David Walker and Sverrir Olafsson. Again, our thanks to our editors at Thorsons, Carole Tonkinson and Elizabeth Hutchins, for making this book possible.

'This Be the Verse' from *Collected Poems* by Philip Larkin, © 1988, 1989, the estate of Philip Larkin, is reprinted by permission of Farrar, Strauss and Giroux, LLC, and Faber & Faber Ltd.

Most of all we would like to thank our wives, Debbie Prior and Jill O'Connor, for their inspiration, support and love

# Introduction
## Joseph O'Connor

■ When I think of close relationships, my mind travels back to a wet Saturday night and a nightclub in south-west London. I was living in a flat at the time. There was a timber yard on one side, which started work very early in the morning, and an expanse of open park on the other. I shared the flat with two friends. One was Max, who would never answer the door to the postman in case he was tricked into accepting a solicitor's letter from his ex-wife. I don't know what he feared, but I have never seen a grown man so afraid of a postman. If the postman rang with a parcel or special delivery, Max would hide and send one of us down with strict instructions: 'Remember, don't accept any recorded delivery letters for me.' My other flatmate was Jack, whose main ambition in life was to get a woman to fall in love with him.

That particular Saturday evening, Max was out with his girlfriend and Jack and I wanted to go out, meet women and enjoy ourselves. A nightclub was the obvious place to go to do all three. A 20-stone bull-necked bouncer turned us away from the first one. I did not appreciate his barring us at the time, but with hindsight I am very glad he did. Strange how life's direction can hinge on such mundane events. However, at the time neither Jack nor I was feeling very philosophical. The streets were drab, with grey puddles in the gutters that seemed to absorb the yellow light from the sodium lamps rather than reflect it. It was late and a thin autumn drizzle had started when we reached the second club. We agreed we would go home if we were turned away from this one, but we got in. I mostly remember the immediate contrast with the streets outside. Inside there was an uproar of colour, movement, light and darkness. And music. Loud music. There were a few corners where you could have a conversation without bellowing really close to your partner's ear, small whirlpools of words in a sea of music. I could tell where they were because all the people who were not dancing were packed into them. A disc jockey in the corner was keeping the music going with a small console and several large speakers.

Jack and I had gone in opposite directions. I was wandering around, having successfully bought a drink, when I saw her. Some inner voices piped up immediately.

'She's why you are here.'

'Go on, she's beautiful. Ask her to dance.'

'She might say no.'

'She might say yes.'

'What about the girlfriend she is dancing with? I can't just butt in.'

'Then wait for a gap in the music.'

'There's a chap over there who is interested as well.'

'Then you had better be quick. What are you waiting for?'

'What about playing it cool?'

'And risk getting frozen out?'

I did ask her to dance. Jack danced with her girlfriend.

I talked to her. Jack talked to her girlfriend.

I made a date to see her again. We married a year later.

Within that previous short sentence there hides 12 long months where we built our relationship, with its pains and pleasures and its setbacks and surprises. During that time we got to know each other, engaging in a dance that was far more subtle and significant than the one that brought us together on the dance floor in the nightclub.

We celebrate our wedding anniversary, of course, and I remember the date of our first meeting and I inwardly celebrate that anniversary too.

And what was it like for my wife at that first meeting? The story is not complete without both points of view. When we talked about it much later, she said the meeting was not significant for her at all at the time. She was in the habit of going to a nightclub with her girlfriends on a Friday night and was not bothered about whether anyone asked her to dance or not. She had two other boyfriends at the time, so she was not looking for a new man in her life. She did not dance with every man who asked her, only those who passed a test that she applied without thinking about it. He had to be both slim and tall. I passed that immediate visual test and also the more demanding test on the first date – to be interesting to talk to. We all evaluate prospective partners on certain measures, sometimes by sight or by hearing and feeling, and that is one subject we will explore in this book.

For most of us, sexual and intimate relationships give us the greatest pleasure and can give us the greatest pain. Driven by our biology and instinct, tempered by our social and cultural upbringing, calmed every so often by the composed voice of the intellect, we dance through life with many partners who are also responding to their own inner voices. I can recognize those parts of myself and I know them quite well now. I can track what they whisper to me about what I should and shouldn't do, what I want to do and what it would be a good idea to do. No one of them holds the answer. And while I can write about them at a distance, in the heat of the moment it is not easy to know what to do. For we have many voices – biological, social and intellectual – and yet relationships are emotional. We feel. We care. That was what pulled me across the dance floor those years ago.

I have remembered some other lessons too. I can never know what happens for the best in advance. The only way I find out is to act. We may or may not recognize those significant points in our life when one door closes and another door opens that leads somewhere we really want to go. And while it is easy to talk of voices, beliefs and values, in the moment of decision, we embody them. What we do is what counts. Afterwards, reason may shuffle the cards and arrange them in a way that makes sense to us whatever happens.

Every day we create and re-create our relationships and we have more choice than sometimes appears. The better we understand ourselves and our beliefs, and the better we understand our partners, the more satisfying and pleasurable relationships we can create.

# Introduction
## Robin Prior

■ I can't remember when my internal voice arrived. It was certainly early in life. Until then I just did things without thought. It may have come as part of a package with my measles, mumps or milk teeth. I remember it was there when I started school, telling me what to put in my satchel and how to flick paper pellets without being caught. Naïvely, I thought I was the only person ever to be given such a voice, in the way that some children have make-believe friends only they can see and talk to. I felt it made me special.

This voice began small, as I did, and whispered in my ear like my grandfather's tame budgerigar. Once in place, it aged with me, giving me advice about everything, even when I did not want it – where to go, whom to talk to, what to do and what I could achieve. It had an opinion to give on every aspect of my life and it talked constantly. It dictated whom I fell in love with and with whom I could have affairs. It was an independent operator and never took the blame for love that went wrong. Broken hearts and unsatisfactory relationships were my responsibility. On that score, it was always silent.

I treated this voice as a guide who would help me do what was best for me. However, over the years, having experienced the consequences of repeated mistakes, I suspected it might not know all that I thought it knew. Although its intentions were well founded, I detected that it was prone to mistakes. I began to challenge it. It was artful in response, parrying my challenges like an expert swordsman, always with an excuse or explanation.

As I listened more intently I noticed that I did not have just the one voice, but a host of them, and they would argue with each other inside my head until one dominated. They tumbled like laundry in a washing machine, wrapping their arms around each other, moving and changing patterns quickly, contradicting each other and leaving me not knowing where one started and another finished.

Knowing these voices represent different aspects of myself, I now understand much more why and where past relationships have gone right and wrong. I now know what makes relationships work for me and the person I am with. And I know how to support my children so they can have relationships that will bring more pleasure than pain and make their lives bigger rather than smaller.

So, what are these voices? How are they different? Let me go back to a warm evening with music playing. I was at a party and saw a girl more beautiful than I thought possible. The sight of her set me on autopilot. I became hot, my heart began to beat fast, the sounds in the room became distant and my vision blurred. Everything became fuzzy and dull except this girl. I needed to meet her as I had needed nothing before and there was nobody going to stand in my way. I was a bull snorting, a stallion scraping its hoof and a gorilla beating its chest – and with enough passion left over to run a marathon. People were talking but I did not hear them. Intent filled my body like hot steel. A voice in my ear gave a clear message: 'She's yours, go get her.' The voice came from the pit of my stomach. It was a hard, determined, almost ruthless voice with a texture I could almost feel. It seemed deep blue in colour and as hot as steam.

Then another man went up to my girl and I felt my heart sink to the floor as anger rose to my head. How could he intrude on what was mine? He had set foot on my territory. I became even hotter. I watched with disbelief and fury as this man and my girl struck up an instant rapport. She was laughing at his jokes. She blushed as he spoke.

Then my instinctive voice left and another voice came into my head with heavy rumblings of doom, reminding me of my place in this world. It told me how relatively unattractive I was and what I could achieve with women. 'Stunning girls like this are not interested in steady men like you,' the voice said in the tones of my early life. This patronizing voice was an amalgam of everyone who had ever known what was best for me. It re-established my limitations. It wanted to look after me and do what was best for me and not expose me to situations where I might get hurt. It spoke quickly and made me feel weak. It crackled with criticism, putting me down, keeping me under control and out of harm's way.

The next morning I lay in bed listening to good old common sense taking the microphone from the other two and sorting me out as usual.

Disappointment was put aside. I took a deep breath and thought of blue skies and gentle seas. I thought about the future, what I had to offer, and I remembered the people who told me I was attractive without being flashy. The path to success, it reminded me, was strewn with disappointment. I realized that many girls were interested in status in the way that men were preoccupied by good looks and at that time I had no status to display or trade on. I acknowledged again that I could not be attractive to all women and that I was better forming relationships with females who would value my qualities. This calm, unemotional voice helped me think through what had happened and come to rational realizations uncluttered by passion or emotion. It was like having Mr Spock from *Star Trek* on my side.

That episode demonstrates the three voices that have influenced the relationships I have formed. First, my basic, genetic drive – the instinct and impulses I experience. Secondly, what I learned to believe was true about myself and the world as I grew up. And thirdly, my intellect and common sense. Although they are separate, these voices almost never operate totally on their own. They change places and intertwine like spaghetti on a plate. None of them can work without influence from the others, yet they can all take over in a second.

Since becoming familiar with my own three voices I have noticed that others have them too. I had an affair years ago with a woman newly separated from her husband. When we were together she would become overwhelmed with passion while constantly saying, 'I shouldn't be doing this.' What I could see told me she wanted to be with me. What I heard told me the opposite. Her instinctive voice was driving what she did and her conditioned voice was driving what she said.

One cold winter's morning, we had a coffee in a small restaurant. People passed by outside, wrapped in coats, shoulders hunched as if trying to slip underneath the icy wind, unaware of the calmly expressed intensity of emotion that we passed across that chequered tablecloth. It was almost surreal, we two caught in this bubble of delicate and fragile feelings, shaping our future as if it were wet clay in our hands, while outside it was only the weather and jobs that mattered. My lady friend had thought her life through and was going to make it work with her husband. Her three voices had agreed on letting her common sense dictate her way forward. Although I was attracted to her and liked being with her, I could see she had made the right decision. My common sense said goodbye to her. But as I said farewell my instinctive voice shouted that I was an idiot and reminded me of the pleasure and intimacy that I was walking away from.

As you read this you may already have some ideas on which of these three voices has the greatest influence on the relationships that you form. You might be the sort of person who is mainly driven by instinctive attraction and so might listen to your genetic voice the most. You might be limited by beliefs about yourself or the opposite sex that stop you fully being with someone. You might be too logical and without romance and have Mr Spock as a constant companion. Or you might have the voices singing in harmony.

Whatever your current relationship and understanding of your internal voices, this book is designed to help you know them better and understand how they influence your relationships. Successful relationships involve working with our genetic and instinctive inclinations, having beliefs, values and a self-image that support successful relationships, and a level of common sense that does not take the fun out of being with another person. Then your three voices will be singing in harmony. Then you can allow your relationships to be what you want them to be.

## NEURO-LINGUISTIC PROGRAMMING

We will be using some ideas from Neuro-Linguistic Programming (NLP) to explore relationships, because NLP is about how we create our own unique subjective world with all its pains and pleasures. NLP began with 'modelling' – how do people do what they do? How do the best communicators get their results? What do they do that is different? We can rephrase these questions to apply to relationships. How do you create a satisfying relationship? What do people who enjoy good relationships do that is different?

NLP can help us understand ourselves and others and we will show many ways to improve your relationships, but relationships are such a big issue that this book goes some way beyond NLP in its scope.

You do not need to have any knowledge of NLP to enjoy and use this book.

# Our Instinctive Voice

## WOMEN DANCE BACKWARDS

Robin sat in a bar recently pretending to read a newspaper and listened to a group of well dressed, well spoken, apparently well educated men sorting out the world. It took them about 10 minutes to find a solution to their company's woes, another five minutes to vent their frustration at being too junior to put their plans into action and another 20 minutes to develop a strategy to fix the world's economic difficulties. Then they started talking about women. That topic took a bit longer. This long deliberation was due, according to them, to female inconsistency rather than their own inability to empathize and understand.

Although they had had a few drinks and the clarity of their conversation declined every round, they were certain there was not a man alive who could understand how a woman's mind worked. And there was not a woman who would ever be able to understand a man. Following another half hour of heated debate which degenerated into a critical assessment of all females, one very demonstrative man waved his hands about and said, as though he had stumbled upon the ultimate truth, 'And do you know the worst thing about women? Well, I'll tell you what the worst thing about women is. I've heard them talking at their coffee mornings. Whenever they get together all they do is bitch about men.'

It is obvious that men and women are different. That has been openly acknowledged since we hunted with spears, apart from a couple of decades this century when in our efforts to acknowledge men and women as equal we have forgotten that people can be different and equal as well. The works of Shakespeare and other great writers show how differently men and women respond to situations. The way laws have been made, the right to vote and many other social, political and legal examples demonstrate that historically not only have men and women been recognized as different, but they have been deemed – by many men – to be unequal. Physical size has given men the right to dominate in most human fields, even those where size is a handicap.

As a young child Robin asked his mother why there were mummies and daddies. Probably fearing a question about the facts of life, she said that mummies had long hair and danced backwards. Even then, Robin knew that did not answer his question, and what was more, she said it in a way that left him feeling that there was much more to discover.

Many people see men and women as being like chalk and cheese, or oil and water, forever incompatible, forced together with the greatest of pleasure for reproductive reasons only. Certainly our biological instincts and drives have a major influence on the relationships we form. As part of our genetic inheritance we seek sex, not only for pleasure but also at a deeper level to continue the species, to leave our mark in the world through our children. Sex is one way we can achieve immortality. But finding a mate is often portrayed as an act of cunning and manipulation, a combination of stealth and enticement in pursuit of someone you wished you could do without – man the hunter and woman the prey.

## Primitive Man

It is worth seeing how our history still influences our behaviour in close relationships. In a primitive Stone Age world, it was more practical for men and women to specialize in various skills and attitudes. There was no point in duplicating effort – the world was a dangerous place, food was not a right, or even guaranteed, and getting lost didn't mean having to buy a map, but risking being killed by animals or your human enemies.

Now the world is very different. Ironically, many of the aspects that made men and women specialists are now working against us, making it harder, not easier to build relationships that meet our needs now and in the future. Survival is now easy. Infant mortality is a small fraction of what it was. Life is a right; now we are only concerned with its quality. We want more, different challenges and other means of satisfaction. To achieve this we need relationships that are not standing knee deep in the mud of primitive demands. Yet in some ways we still wear our Stone Age furs under our smart twentieth-century clothes. They itch, especially in the company of the opposite sex. Somehow we have to deal with the feelings shaped by thousands of years of evolution in one short lifetime.

## Hard Wiring

With all of the excellent and illuminating work currently being carried out on genetics, we are now more aware of the influence our 'hard wiring' has on our behaviour. We are now able to view obesity, disease, violence, sexual orientation and other variations from the popular 'norm' as being something that individuals may carry in their bodies. Genetics can help society take a different, and hopefully more fruitful, approach to many social problems. It is the study of genetics that has given us permission to say men and women are different.

However, the danger with the study of genetics is that it provides an easy excuse and justification for behaviour we know to be anti-social. Men commit 82 per cent of recorded crime in the United Kingdom. This fact is common knowledge throughout the police force and is instrumental in the planning of prisons. Men commit an even higher percentage of violent crime. These figures have changed little over the last 30 years and are replicated in most other parts of the world. It is true that social conditioning plays a big part in this imbalance of criminal behaviour between men and women. However, the evidence and the research suggest that there is a genetic basis to much of this anti-social behaviour.

What then? Do we then throw up our hands in defeat and say, 'Well that's the way men are, so let them get on with it.' That would be absurd. Many people, however, are throwing up their hands and saying, 'This is how I am meant to be and there's nothing I can do about it,' when it is obvious that what they are doing suits only themselves. If you want your relationships to flounder, then just blame your faults on your masculine or feminine genes. (And blame other people's faults on their gender too.)

Civilization might be seen as the process and the result of channelling and controlling those instinctual drives for the greater good – the greater good being the survival and happiness of everyone, because ultimately we are social, we cannot live without others. So, even though we still carry this 'hard wiring', there is no excuse for letting the monkey within us keep us in the jungle. And if men and women are 'hard wired' differently, this is wonderful. 'Differently' does not mean better or worse, superior or inferior. When men and women come together in a satisfying relationship, this is a celebration of difference. Let us enjoy the difference. Let us build the team for the future, making the most of our genetic inheritance.

## THE THREE VOICES

Our genetically driven instinctive voice is a joy. It makes us feel alive. It fills us with passion and gives us pleasure. It turns our head when someone beautiful walks into the room. It tickles our ears when we hear an attractive voice of the opposite sex. It gives us joy in the arms of our lovers.

Secondly, there is the voice of civilization, the social voice. It comes from the society and culture that we live in. This voice conditions us to live in our society. While the message is from society as a whole, the main messengers are our parents. They also add all sorts of other messages of their own, like a cultural game of Chinese whispers.

The conditioning voice can drown out many others. It affects our beliefs, values, thoughts and actions. Part of the work of becoming mature is to go beyond the limiting messages and influences of first our parents, then our society, then our culture, to a place where we can feel at home in the world, not just in our neighbourhood.

Thirdly, there is the voice of our intellect. Calm and steady on its own, it tells us what makes sense.

Both men and women have these three voices. They may have a different balance or sequence for each of us. They may whisper slightly different messages in different tones.

The first challenge of forming satisfying relationships is to accommodate the energy of the genetic voice. It is deeper than the social, sometimes manifests violently and can be disruptive. The second challenge is to find a place for the social voice so that it does not deaden the joy and energy of the genetic voice. The third challenge is to accommodate the intellect, because we have a life outside our close relationships as well. Ultimately, we hope to achieve a state of passion tempered by society and guided by reason.

The key to a successful relationship is knowing your own three voices, your partner's voices, and working together to make all six sing in harmony.

So, do good relationships mean an uneasy compromise between nature and nurture? Not necessarily. Not unless the instinctive voice is the only one that you pay attention to. Our genes are only one influence on how we relate to others. Genetic differences will only inhibit how we are with each other if we want them to do so. In the way that a knife can be used to carve fine furniture or to stab someone, our genetic drives may be used to bring shared pleasure or to keep ourselves apart.

Why are we looking at relationships using these three voices and not just taking relationships as a whole? It is because putting a subject into a larger context and then examining its component parts allows us greater knowledge. With that knowledge we can see how the parts combine to make a harmonious relationship. Then we can understand ourselves and others better. With greater understanding, we can make our relationships more satisfying.

If we look at tennis, for example, in the broader context of competitive sport we can better understand the motivation, attraction and the role that it fulfils. We can then look at the different players, styles and roles involved to understand how the details build up to the whole.

So, if we then look at the different complementary parts that make a relationship work (or not), we can then gain a better understanding of how the whole can be improved. We can identify which of these component parts provides the strengths and weaknesses of being together.

Understanding our own three voices will also help us understand ourselves as a whole. The genetic voice is not the villain of the piece, unless we let it be so. If we harness our genetic drives to build the relationship that we and our partner want, they will hold us together, stop either party straying and build a bond that will enable us both to grow and have the life we want. Being in relationships that work is not rocket science – it is far more important than rocket science.

## RELATIONSHIPS GOOD AND BAD

I (Robin), remember that during the First World War, my grandfather was in charge of a horse-drawn wagon to carry ammunition from the arsenal to where it was needed on the front line. He was only 16 and too young to fight, although he was old enough to be killed. One day he was sitting with his wagon, which was being loaded with ammunition to take to the troops at the height of the battle. Amid all the torrent of noise, the smoke and stench of warfare, his normally obedient horse reared up and bolted, taking him and the wagon with it. Seconds later a German shell exploded where my grandfather and his psychic horse had been waiting a moment before.

My grandfather maintained until the day he died of old age that the horse heard the shell coming through the air, singled it out from all the other shells exploding and took evasive action. Whether the horse heard the shell or not, its bolting saved my grandfather and, by today's count, 37 descendants.

One of his lineage is obviously me, a man with a great affection for horses that bolt. And I have three daughters. Each one began because one sperm out of 280 million fertilized a particular egg. Had another sperm been a better swimmer than the one that won the race, my daughters would be different. My two younger daughters only exist because I stumbled over my wife-to-be's suitcase in the lobby of a hotel. Had I not turned without thinking or had she not put her suitcase where she had, we would never have spoken. If you examine the unlikely sequence of events that led to you being who you are, where you are, reading this book, it makes winning the lottery seem like an odds-on bet. And what point is there to winning such an elusive prize and then not using it? Being born is a once in a lifetime opportunity. And probably the most important influence on the quality of your life is the relationships that you form.

So, what influence do relationships have on your life? What is the point in putting effort into making them work? To find out, try this thought experiment.

Think of two relationships in particular, one good and one not so good. If you do not have an example of one or both of these, then make them up for the sake of the exercise.

First, take the relationship that was not so good. Remember that and mentally put yourself back with that person.

Close your eyes, imagine being back with that person. Do not see yourself in the picture, but see them as if through your own eyes, as if you were back there now.

Picture them as clearly as you can. See their complexion, the colour of their eyes and hair. Picture the places you used to meet.

Now hear their voice and the sort of conversations that you had and hear any associated sounds. Then, listen to your internal voice. Is it saying anything?

Now notice what feelings you have and where those feelings are located in your body.

Are they light or heavy?
Does your energy level rise or fall?
Is your breathing affected?

Now, carry forward these sounds, pictures and feelings, and, in the frame of mind that you have just created, think about the future and what life could be like for you.

Now, take a deep breath and shake off that frame of mind. Get rid of the pictures, sounds and feelings.

Now, repeat the process, putting yourself this time into the better relationship. Imagine being with that person.

See them in your mind's eye as if you were back with them.
Remember what you saw, what you heard and anything your internal
voice said, and notice how you feel.
Re-create the scenes, recall the sort of conversations you had.
Be inside yourself experiencing this memory.
Build up this experience until the memory becomes as lifelike as you can
make it.

How does this positive experience influence your frame of mind for the
future?

---

This simple exercise will show you the influence positive relationships
can have on the way you are and how the future can be. A poor
relationship clouds the future; a good one illuminates it. A poor relationship saps your energy and a good one gives you energy. A relationship is a major influence on your whole emotional state and this state
of mind influences how you see the world, your levels of enthusiasm
and what you believe to be possible.

## THE SURVIVAL OF THE MOST FITTING

The genetic voice usually gives the initial impetus in forming sexual
relationships. It is part of the instinctual knowledge we are born with in
order to survive. Babies know how to suck the breast, cry for help and
scream when they are soiled. They naturally stimulate their parents' loving and caring instincts, even when the parents are stumbling around
the house like zombies from lack of sleep. Babies know how to smile
when only a few weeks old to trigger love in a mother fatigued by constant caring. This parental loving and caring is also part of our instinct
to a greater or lesser degree. I (Joseph) remember looking into the eyes of
my newly born daughter and seeing into the centre of the world, deep
and still. It was like seeing into human nature before society had
changed it. I was enchanted. It was like looking into a very clear pool,
yet not seeing the bottom. Our instincts go high as well as deep.

Most of the time these genetic instincts are unconscious. They are
effortless. Sometimes it takes effort to deny them. Yet they come with
being born.

Our genetic knowledge has evolved with us. Genes are the tools of evolution. They are the units of inheritance, millions and millions on every chromosome, 46 chromosomes in every cell in our body. They are the hard-wired, bred in the bone instructions passed from one generation to the next, telling them what sort of offspring to produce. They influence everything – size, colouring, strength, resistance to disease, reproductive capabilities and intellect.

The passing on of genes was understood long before the word itself had been invented. Friends and relatives have argued for generations about the physical characteristics inherited by babies. They have looked at a scrunched up bawling bundle of humanity and noticed similarities between its bud of a nose and that of its 90-year-old great-grandmother.

I (Joseph) was on holiday with my family in Boulder, Colorado, many years ago. Our daughter Lara was about two-and-a-half years old. We were walking downtown where there were many pavement artists and Lara wanted to have her portrait drawn. She picked an artist who did caricatures. He drew her eating a hamburger. It only took a few minutes. He stepped back and showed me the picture. Lara was delighted. I looked at the picture. There, staring out from the paper, was my mother-in-law! The resemblance was uncanny. All the artist had done was accentuate a feature here, bring out a certain look and the family resemblance was striking. I still have the portrait.

Genetic messages that work positively and are compatible with the environment survive, or, more accurately, they increase the chance of survival for the person who has them. Those that do not work decrease the chance of survival of those who carry them; they slowly diminish from one generation to the next until they are gone.

As environments change, so different genes acquire survival value. Darwin called this process 'survival of the fittest', although it may be more easily understood as the survival of the 'most fitting' – those who are most suited to the environment they inhabit. Being the biggest, fastest or strongest does not always make you the fittest, as the dinosaurs found out. Nor are genes simple carriers, one per feature. They work together, just as evolution is more like co-evolution of species balancing and needing each other to survive in the dance of life.

## The Swiftest Gazelle

Evolution is normally slow. Our Neolithic ancestor who hauled the stones to make Stonehenge over 4,500 years ago was genetically almost the same as modern man. The world, however, is now very different from the one in which he laboured.

Evolution is also paradoxically selfish. Although survival or reproduction of the fittest benefits the group to which it belongs, the individual's concern is for the individual. The best way to ensure the group's survival is to make sure each individual survives. When a gazelle runs away from a lion, it tries to outrun the lion, of course, but it also seeks to outrun other gazelles. The lion gets the sick, the weak and the slowest runners. The fittest gazelles survive and the group prospers, but this is small consolation to the gazelle that ends its life as the lion's dinner. The survival of the fittest and the genetic prosperity of the group are the result of everyone looking after their own interests. Humans sometimes work against survival of the fittest – we go back and rescue the sick and the weak who are threatened.

According to the laws of evolution, our main objective as men and women is to ensure that our *own* genes are passed on. One primitive male strategy to achieve this objective is to impregnate as many females as possible. This is also a strategy based on quantity – a million sperm per ejaculation means that men can father many children. To control his mates and keep them away from other males, he needs to dominate territory. The stronger the man, the better his pick of the women. A female strategy is based on quality – to care well for the relatively few children she can have. In order to provide shelter for her children, the female needed the male around. She evolved a sense of relationship that the male had less evolutionary pressure to match.

So, on a *purely genetic* level, the male needs territory, possession, the certainty of fatherhood and the knowledge that his children will be well cared for. The female needs strong survival genes for the children, shelter and protection. These drives are still alive and well in us. They still influence whom we choose to mate with and we need to acknowledge them, while realizing they are not the whole story.

## The Chemistry Between Us

We are also physically 'hard wired' in a certain way. Men are under the influence of the male hormone testosterone. This is what helps to build muscular strength. It also makes men more aggressive. It is a powerful influence on sexual thinking and behaviour. Women who are given testosterone injections for medical reasons often complain that they are thinking about sex very frequently. To which men reply, 'Sure, isn't that normal?'

The female equivalent hormone is oxytocin. It is the hormone that stimulates childbirth and is used to induce delivery. It has the interesting side-effect of creating amnesia. It also brings very strong feelings of relationship, nurturing and caring. So, is the answer to relationship problems simply to give men injections of oxytocin? No, because it does not fit in with the rest of their hormones. Testosterone is one way evolution makes men protect, explore and defend their territory. Oxytocin is one way evolution makes sure that children are nurtured, protected and cared for. From the biological point of view, children don't need two mothers or two fathers, ideally they need one of each.

There is now a whole field of research, known as evolutionary psychology, that studies the effects of biological evolution on psychological traits. What it seems to show is that men and woman have very different values and move in different directions because of the way they have evolved. Men tend towards the values of individuality, justice, rights and activity. Women tend more towards valuing relationship and everything connected with it, including care and responsibility.

Just as men and women are not the same, no two men are the same and no two women are the same. There is a danger in generalization, taking a type of behaviour, aptitude or attitude that we think is common to a group of people and then applying it to the whole group, irrespective of individual variation.

What we have all evolved is a variety of stratagems when it comes to attracting a partner or being attractive to a partner, including trickery, enticement, coercion, force, posturing, preening, posing and conflict. These ways of behaving are common throughout the animal world, because they work and so they are passed on to the next generation. Evolution selects those of both sexes with the greatest ingenuity and guile as well as other attributes. Indeed, many popular magazine articles offering help in relationships focus on the skills of enticement, entrapment and coercion. Neolithic man and woman would be quite at home browsing airport news stands.

## Teamwork

As human beings evolved, men and women who specialized by taking different roles achieved higher levels of expertise, flourished and had more offspring. Those who worked as a team 'outran' those who did not. This teamwork stemmed from the common goal of survival in order to reproduce.

For many thousands of years couplings based on these primitive needs worked. Primitive technology gave them shelter, heat in the winter and food for their offspring. With aspirations limited by the level of technology and opportunity, demands on the partner were limited. The greater the expectation and possibilities of life, then the greater the expectation of the partner. Over the last century, our way of life and the pressures upon male and female relationships have changed more than ever before, yet our natural drives have remained the same. Our instinctive voice helps us choose partners for today based on survival criteria from many thousands of years ago.

What we can do is bring about our own 'accelerated adaptation' by working with our genetic drives. We can enjoy and wallow in the pleasures that these drives provide while applying our intellect to handle those that do not contribute to life now. We know we no longer need big territories. We can design a relationship for our future that takes into account our instinctive desires, how the world has changed and what we intellectually know will work.

Evolution is not only slow, it has no destination. If it seems to have a direction, it is one that we read into it from our privileged position at the top of the food chain. There is no final plan, certainly not one in which human beings must be a part. Getting it right is up to us.

## NATURE VERSUS NURTURE

It can be hard to separate instinct from learned behaviour. Our actions are the result and combination of the two and so are our differences. Much of our conditioning is born out of genetic differences. It is a truism that boys are given soldiers and footballs to play with while girls are given dolls and clothes. So conditioning tends to reinforce the tendencies that are already there from our biology. However it would be just as stupid to make girls have the guns and boys the dolls – every child should have the chance to choose their individual way of embodying their gender.

Also, people often look to the parents to know how to treat the children. I (Joseph) look rather like my father physically and therefore I had many people telling me how like him in character I was. They assumed physical likeness meant character likeness. So I was told I was artistic, musical and impractical. It took some time to differentiate between my own qualities and those merely attributed to me by well-meaning people. I decided to develop my artistic and musical talents, but in a practical way. Also, because my father is an actor, my school-teachers assumed I could act as well and it took toe-clenchingly bad performances in the school play three years running to persuade them otherwise.

I (Robin) have only the faintest of memories of my father, who died when I was five. When I was young I was inundated by well-meaning people telling me what a pleasant and caring man he was. They also continually noted how physically like him I was. Without doubt, even though I have no memory of it, I must have learned some behaviour from him. The pressure of being compared to him must also have shaped some of my behaviour. I looked like him, therefore I must act like him. People now know me as a pleasant and caring man. But how much of my character has been inherited in my genes and how much is learned behaviour it is impossible to say.

One of the great difficulties in separating learned behaviour from genetically inherited characteristics is that we tend to get them both from the same source. If you believe that some of the characteristics referred to in this chapter are learnt rather than genetically inherited, then that is fine. Learning may reinforce, override or work together with instinctual behaviour.

## The Family Unit

With sperm banks, artificial insemination, cloning and various other ways of propagating the species becoming increasingly available there is a question about the validity or necessity of the traditional family unit. Studies suggest the children of one-parent families seem to be disadvantaged, although that might be part of society's learning process. Society is still organized to favour the traditional family unit. It is possible that in the future we can become organized in such a way that one-parent families thrive more than traditional family units.

Whatever the form of the family group to which we belong, we want satisfying and happy relationships. We want to feel secure and loved, and give security and love in return, However, nature still appears to want us to form couples. Evolutionists suggest that the two-parent family has been and will probably continue to be the most efficient model for creating and raising children. By the time people reach maturity, the population is split almost equally between men and women. Birth rates are slightly higher for boys, however. There are roughly 106 boys born in the Western world for every 100 girls. This compensates to a degree for the higher levels of child mortality in boys. It might also reflect the male's traditional (and more risky) role of hunter, protector and warrior. Indeed, it appears that after the heavy loss of males such as occurred during the First World War, more boy babies were born, supposedly to restore the balance. How did nature 'know'? There are deeper forces at work than our conscious intelligence.

There is a myth in many traditions that man and woman were originally one whole person which was split apart. Consequently each is forever trying to be reunited with the lost half. 'My other half' is still a phrase people use for their partner. The Christian myth of Adam and Eve has the same idea behind it.

Many people who divorce or separate go on to marry for a second or third time. This suggests that we want to be part of a couple but we do not always get it right first time.

So why hasn't evolution made the male and female bond stronger? Unlike swans, which die of a broken heart when their partner dies, people are deemed by evolution to be too precious to waste. Therefore, we bond slightly less strongly than some species, but very much more strongly than others, allowing either partner to form new relationships if their partner dies. That is fine and understandable. This ability to begin again without feelings of guilt towards a lost partner allows people to make the most of their lives.

## STEREOTYPES AND DIFFERENCES

Evolution pushes us into the future through our children. Once we have children, then as far as evolution is concerned, our main purpose is to keep them healthy until they reach adulthood. This is the minimum that is expected of parents; of course we do much more. The parental burden on humanity is far greater than on any other species. If we look back only a few generations, when life expectancy was lower and families larger than now, you will find people whose entire adult lives carried parental responsibility. There was no retirement from family commitments apart from death. To make parenting easier, men and women specialized in different functions. These mental and physical capabilities still affect how we approach day-to-day activities now and how we seek out and treat partners. These differences can be very fulfilling – but they can also wreck our relationships. The purpose in looking at genetic difference is to understand the team of the past in order to shape the team of the future.

Nature has two sexes for very good reasons, mainly as the most efficient way of spreading differences in the population. To say that men and women are different does not pass a value judgement on either. Men are on average stronger than women. That doesn't make strength a virtue and men more virtuous than women. All it means is that most men are stronger than most women. Sometimes strength is useful, sometimes not. What is important is how that difference affects the relationship between us. If any difference is used to force a partner into a role they do not want, then that is wrong, be it applied by a man or a woman.

There are common stereotypes of men and women. They crop up on television, newspapers, films and conversations. We have exaggerated them but slightly. You will no doubt have heard variations of them.

According to one stereotype, all men are bullies who think only of themselves. All they are interested in is football, beer and sex, preferably in that order. They are untidy and dirty, and they never remember birthdays, anniversaries or where they left their car keys. Women trust them and take them into their confidence at their peril. Given half a chance or half a pint, the man will spill the confidences at the local public house. Men, in short, behave badly. They suffer from testosterone poisoning, turning from angelic choirboys into surly Neanderthals almost overnight. Men, to quote Woody Allen, have been given both a penis and a brain, but only enough blood to operate one of them at a time. Enough.

Let us keep the balance of the sexes by giving the other stereotype. Women love doing the housework and having coffee mornings with their friends. Their greatest joys are shopping and talking and they are consummately good at both. The only time they show any interest in sex is if another woman takes an interest in their man. They are happiest when they are pregnant and men should never ask them to take a rational decision. They are not logical and jump from one subject to another at the drop of a hat; they cannot follow an argument. They suffer from oxytocin poisoning.

To sum up in the words of Aldous Huxley: 'Women minus men equals lunatic, men minus women equals pig.' Or, in the words of the American comedian Billy Crystal, 'Women need a reason to make love, men need a place.'

These stereotypes are annoying, aren't they? They are caricatures, but worse. No person is like that, although they contain a drop of truth in an ocean of blindness.

Stereotypes take the extreme view, but any generalization can make you blind to an individual's good or bad points. If your experience is that members of the opposite sex are loving and you assume that all people of that sex will therefore be loving, an individual who does not love may hurt you. Likewise, if you think all members of the opposite sex have a specific weakness or fault, you may be blind to the individual who is not like that. We often see what we expect to see. Yet we are all unique and should be treated as such.

## Some Generalizations

A caveat before we start – these are generalizations from a biological perspective only. Also, there are always exceptions to generalizations otherwise they would not be generalizations, they would be rules. However, in the way that we can say men are heavier than women without meaning all men are heavier than all women, we may make some observations about the genders to help mutual understanding. Here are some generalizations that seem well founded on present research studies.

Boys show more vigorous limb movement during their early development. As toddlers, male children like to hammer toys and gain their understanding of things by breaking them. They are far more robust and climb more than girls. They are rougher, more violent and noisily exuberant than girls. They are far more boisterous. Girls are quicker to speak, read, learn and understand human interactions. They are academically more advanced than boys and have a higher average intelligence level.

The additional size of the male continues throughout life. Men are on average 20 per cent heavier than females and 30 per cent stronger. However, the size differential is now measurably smaller than it used to be, which suggests that evolution is playing its part in shaping the male of the future. With this additional size, men are far more physically aggressive. They have a history of fighting. And there is no concrete evidence that the meek will inherit the Earth (unless the strong surrender without a fight).

Females, on the other hand, are less vulnerable to disease than men. From the biological point of view, the father is more dispensable as long as the mother is around to nurture a child. Women carry more body fat, a store to help them get through times of famine.

Men have larger noses to take in more oxygen when fighting. A man's voice deepens with the arrival of higher levels of testosterone at a time when he needs to sound aggressive and fight for his mates. His beard grows to be the equivalent of a lion's mane and a warning sign to other males that there are new genes on the block.

The flood of testosterone in adolescence makes boys anti-social and insular. It makes them want to be alone or with others finding the same need for loneliness. It would seem that historically this anti-social behaviour precipitated them leaving their group and finding a new one in which to fight for females. This would have prevented inbreeding.

Men take greater risks. A substance called MAO has now been identified in the human body; it is linked strongly with risk taking. Men have more MAO than women. Young men have more than old men do. People interested in dangerous sports and activities have more than those involved in more passive and less dangerous pastimes. Dangerous criminals have more than anybody.

Historically men have been the sex that breaks boundaries, comes up with new inventions and discovers new worlds. Much of this adventurous supremacy has been due to the lack of opportunity for females living under the control of men and the lack of accurate reporting. However, there is something in many men that makes them look out to the horizon and yearn to know what exists beyond it. Men like brinkmanship, sailing close to the edge. For it has been the adventurous males who have gained the most mates.

Men see most things as a challenge. They are more competitive. Capitalism is designed for and by men. The sense of urgency in the American space programme appears to have been greater when there were Russians to beat. Young men make the most compliant soldiers. Testosterone seems to influence them in two directions: to either kill or have sex. When the hormones run high, they do not need much justification to fight for a cause. Part of their risk taking is a sense of indestructibility and immortality, which also makes for a good soldier. Older men are more likely to look for an easier way of resolving issues. Perhaps the reduction of MAO and the awareness that others depend on them, together with the realization of their own mortality, makes older men less adventurous.

So instinctive is competition to men that they think it is natural that women should want to watch them play sport. American football, with players exaggerated in size by padding, rushing at each other like bulls, with cheerleaders standing at the side looking like pretty prizes for the victor is, for all to see, a re-enactment of primitive virility performances.

Although team players, men also like to achieve on their own. They like competency, efficiency and achievement. And they need to know they have a purpose. They need to feel needed.

Men are territorial. Space, ground, earth and ownership mean more mates. They also like to mark out their territory in some way, stamp their own identity on it. Indeed, it is believed that when a couple goes into a hotel room the woman tests the bed and the man urinates in the bathroom as a modern re-enactment of their instinctive roles.

Women, on the other hand, see quite clearly the benefits of community, co-operation and relationship. They know how to create peace and harmony. They do not need wars or conflict. They prefer happiness to being right.

Men tend to be better at single activities whereas women are good at multi-tasking. I (Joseph) live with my wife and two daughters and sometimes I feel I am on a fairground roller-coaster as the conversation swings around and turns sharp corners with no connection between subjects – at least to me. 'How does that connect with what we were just talking about?' I will ask helplessly. 'It doesn't,' they reply. 'We thought you'd finished.' I accuse them of jumping around from subject to subject and they say I am not flexible enough to keep up.

Women are better at verbal skills. Not being able to depend on brute force, they have developed greater social awareness and perception. Their senses are sharper. They understand and value relationships more. That is why it is often the female who holds a relationship together. It is also why it is usually the female who ends the relationship, because she can see when it will not work far more quickly than the man can.

When upset or troubled, a man will want to withdraw and mull things over, making sure everyone else knows he is mulling. However, the benefits of being mean, moody and brooding with a spear in your hand are not obvious. Women tend to want to talk things through, thinking as they talk.

So men and women are different. Hardly a novel conclusion. What do we make of that? One poor choice would be to spend our lives determined to get the opposite sex to see things the way we want them to. The same broad principles apply to same-sex relationships. It is self-defeating to try to get your partner to see, hear and feel the same way as you do. This is the way to unhappiness for both sexes. If we take the differences and see how to combine skills and abilities to meet modern needs, we are on our way to a better and more satisfying relationship.

## ATTRACTION AND ATTRACTIVENESS

Initial attraction is immediate and not always based on how a person looks. However, a person who immediately sets our hearts on fire can very easily douse those flames if they do not fit in other respects. There are times, however, such as holidays or while drinking alcohol (both together for the strongest effect), when it takes the other voices a little longer to be heard. Short romances tend to be driven primarily by the instinctive voice. The longer the courtship, the more time the other voices have to give their contribution. However, the longer it takes for your conditioning and common sense to have their say, the greater your investment in time and commitment. You can find yourself with someone stunningly good looking with whom you have nothing in common and no apparent way of getting out of the relationship. In this case your instinctive voice will argue strongly against stopping the relationship.

Genetically driven attraction is important to us because it drives the sex we desire, whereas our conditioning tends to influence the relationships that we form. Generally speaking, and again from the biological perspective, what a man finds physically attractive in a woman are characteristics that represent health. They want a female who looks as if she can supply healthy genes to match his own, is fit enough to survive pregnancy and childbirth, and is able to feed a child on breast milk until he, the male, can provide for the child. If any one of these three criteria is not met, then the chances of the male's genes surviving are reduced. And although, with the use of milk substitutes and medical care, most of the risk has been taken out of pregnancy and birth, the male eye still sparkles when it sees any of the old signs of a suitable partner. Health shows itself in the sheen of the hair, moisture in the skin and a clear sparkle in the eyes. As we age our hair, skin and eyes become drier and more pallid. Biologically, the levels of natural moisture relate directly to fertility.

To the male eye, soft, round curves are also synonymous with health. It is not, however, the case that the more she curves, the more attractive the woman. There is an optimum, a point between not being curvy enough and being too curvy. It is the ratio between hips and weight that is important, not the size of either. In some non-Westernized cultures and periods in European history bigger meant more beautiful. These times do seem to have been when food was less abundant and of poorer quality than now. So being fatter, although increasing the risk of weight-related disease, reduced the chances of malnourishment-related illness. Rubens painted in an age when this was true. Symmetry in face and body is also seen a sign of health and, therefore, is attractive.

Women have instinctive strategies too. They seek out strong genes. Traditionally a handsome man has been one with big muscles, a strong jaw and an aggressive manner. A woman's second criterion is for someone who will provide shelter and food, so that any offspring can be brought up safely and in good health, maximizing their chances of survival. In primitive times these two usually came in the same package. Height, muscles, aggression, strength and the desire to control and dominate normally provided healthy genes and someone jealous enough to keep others away. Intelligence is sexy too. An intelligent man is one who is more likely to have a well paid job and so be a good provider and protector.

The need for protection goes with the desire for power, position, status and influence in a male partner. As Chairman Mao's wife said, 'First there was sex and then there was power.' The fact that power is sexy goes with the male desire to compete and dominate. It is one reason many men strive to achieve and become successful, sometimes at the cost of their health, their friends, their hobbies and, ironically, the family they have acquired while becoming successful.

Women are also attracted to signs of health in the way that men are. However, instead of curves they respond to muscles, though usually not the exaggerated muscularity that you see in body-building competitions.

Women tend to see sexual or romantic attentions as having the potential for a longer-term relationship. For them sex and relationship are more closely connected. They will expect a casual relationship to have the possibility of developing over time. Men may find this expectation confusing and women may find a man's short-term strategy heartless.

There does seem to be a shift taking place in female attraction at the moment. This may be a temporary change, a fashion or aberration. It might be evolution in process or our unconscious move towards accelerated adaptation. But modern male film stars do seem to be softer and more caring than their rough and ready predecessors.

And of course personality is important. Having a sense of humour and being caring, loving, trustworthy and fun are more important attributes than physical appearance and status. Some of these qualities relate directly to the desire for protection. However, many are relevant to the quality of life rather than survival and reproduction. Whereas men see a bright personality as an indication that a woman is in touch with her sensuous side, women seem to be taking attraction onto a higher level.

A great deal of work has been carried out on the influence of natural body smells in attraction. Much of this research comes out of a desire to bottle sexual attraction and make a lot of money. Nothing sells like sex. The research does suggest that when women ovulate, they find the smell of male pheromones more attractive than at other times of the month. It also appears that their own smell changes and men are unknowingly aware of this and are drawn towards it.

Research also suggests that both men and women are drawn to someone of equal physical attraction to themselves. The shared desire to find the most attractive partner creates a levelling out. We find someone who is aesthetically pleasing but not so much so that they could get someone better than us. Indeed, this need for similarity has been known for generations. Adult children bringing home prospective partners to show their parents have been told in no uncertain terms whether or not the person is good enough for them. These instant assessments by protective parents are normally based on physical appearance. When we see men and women together where one is very much more attractive than the other, we assume there has to be something else to balance the equation – money, power or personality.

Remember these are generalizations from only one point of view – the instinctive, biological view. They are not the whole story. Of course there are many other influences in our choice of a partner and social factors and rational thought play their part, yet the instinctive attractions are strong. We are separating these social, instinctive and rational strands at first in order to bring them together later.

Finally, here is a way you can get to know your instinctive voice better.

---

Think back to a time when you were extremely physically attracted to a partner, perhaps by their looks, perhaps by their voice. Never mind what happened afterwards, what is important was that you were attracted, you wanted to get to know them better and you were able to talk to them, even if only for a little while.

What did you see that attracted you?
What was the quality of the other person's voice that attracted you?
When you think of them, what sort of picture do you have?
What are the qualities of that picture?
Is it large or small, bright or dark, moving or still?
Is it in colour or black and white?
How far away does it seem to be?

What sort of sound seems to be associated with the picture?
What, if anything, are you saying to yourself?
What is the quality of your internal voice?
What sort of feelings do you have?
Where are these feelings and what qualities do they have?

These sorts of questions will let you explore the genetic voice, that part of you that is immediately attracted to someone, before you even know them and before you have a chance to let the other voices speak.

---

So, if sexual attraction is based on genetics, is it still important? Of course it is. Should we be resisting instinctive appeal? Of course not. Why resist something that gives so much pleasure? If we ignore the importance instinctive appeal can play in a relationship we are courting disaster. If you are not physically and sexually attracted to a partner at the beginning, it is more difficult for the relationship to grow, even though other forms of attraction may well develop. When you stay in a relationship with someone who does not attract you in any way, then you are setting yourself up to cheat. If that instinctive voice is ignored and put to the back of the cupboard, one day, in a moment of weakness, someone will come along and release the passion in you. Sexual chemistry is necessary to distinguish a romantic relationship from a friendship, even though it satisfies only one of our three voices.

# 2

# Our Conditioned Voice

■ The genetic voice comes with being born, the conditioned voice with growing up in society.

The conditioned voice has three aspects. First, it is part of what makes us human. It is society's message in our ear. It begins from the moment we are born and is usually in our parents' tone of voice. We could also call it 'the social voice'. Ever since Pavlov's experiments 'conditioning' has had a bad press, because it carries the idea of being limited, being controlled by a stimulus. However, the conditioned voice can be limiting or liberating. It is necessary for us to live in society, for it is only by living in society and learning language that we fulfil our potential. However, as we shall see, this comes at a price.

Secondly, the conditioned voice is made up of our cultural beliefs, expectations and world view. This strongly influences how we react to power, deal with authority and view risk, and the roles, responsibilities and rights of men and women.

Lastly, these conditioned messages are relayed through individual people, first family, and then teachers, peers and friends. This is the part of the conditioned voice we are interested in here. This is where the 'conditions' that form the voice are crucial.

## Learning

The conditioned voice is one result of our insatiable desire to learn. Our survival depends on our learning ability. Humans take longer than other animals to reach maturity. We have to learn what other animals know instinctively. This means we are more dependent on adults to care for us and protect us when we are children, but that we have much greater flexibility of thought and action later, from what we learn.

Babies are voracious learners. Just as they will explore and put all sorts of things into their mouths, not always edible, so we also learn many things in the course of growing up, not all of them helpful. When we are children we do not yet have the awareness and the information to make judgements as to what is useful and what is not, therefore much of our conditioning just slips into our heads without being examined. Much of what is gathered is absorbed irrespective of potential for good or harm. Only later, if at all, do we critically examine our legacy of conditioning.

Our parents, environment, culture and upbringing all shape our conditioned voice. Parts of it are passed from one generation to the next like an old audiotape collection. Patterns trickle down the generations. Some conditioning will stop at one level and go no further, whereas much carries on through countless generations. Just go to your high street and see how many shops have the phrase '& son' in their title.

Our conditioning plays a major role in the relationships we form because it strongly influences how we conduct ourselves within those relationships. Our conditioned voice supplies the rules and boundaries that we live by. It tells us who we are supposed to be, what's right and wrong, what's important and what to do.

Our conditioned voice may reinforce instinct or go against it. Usually it opposes it. Strong conditioning can override and suppress genetic drives. Very often our conditioned voice has been shaped by others in order to counteract impulses that stem from our natural and innate drives. When this happens the voices go to war, fighting for supremacy and the right to be heard.

If so much of how we are comes hard wired in, what's the point of having room for learned behaviour and attitudes which have such potential to go wrong?

One of the reasons for this is that we have so much to learn. Only the simplest behaviour can be instinctual; the more complex the behaviour, the more learning needed. Nature trades off a long time in a dependent state for high potential to learn. Learning must be very important if evolution is willing to make this trade. And even when we are adults, learning does not stop. We learn throughout life.

Another reason for us having so much space for learning is the sheer diversity of environments that we live in. If you were born into an Eskimo family with a full set of Eskimo knowledge then emigrated to downtown New York, you might be annoyed to find being the best seal hunter on your block of little help in dodging the traffic. Our capacity to learn enables us to maximize our potential for survival (and hence genetic immortality) wherever we are born. So in one sense we are in a position to shape our own destiny. The downside is that because we are so open to learning, we can learn some strange behaviour, beliefs and values that may hinder us from achieving our full potential.

## OUR WORLD AND WHAT IT MEANS

As we grow we notice that those around us have two arms and two legs, a head, the same number of facial features, talk the same language and eat the same food. It is not surprising, therefore, that we assume that everyone else sees, hears and feels the same way as we do. We assume that everyone else shares our perception of the world and everything in it. We discover they don't the hard way, by repeated misunderstanding. We may have the same senses, but we act on our *interpretations* of what we see hear and feel – what it means to us. And we all make slightly different – sometimes very different – meaning out of our experience. Have you ever wondered what sort of world your partner lives in? It is the same as yours and yet completely different.

What happens is something like this. We respond only to a few of all the possible sights, sounds, smells, tastes and feelings that assail us. There is so much information around us that we could not possibly take it all in. We have to be selective and simplify what we notice otherwise we could not process relevant information. Right now, you are aware of this book and perhaps some background noise. But what of your heartbeat, the shape of your hands and the feel of your fingers? It is easy to become aware of many things, but usually we need a good reason to direct our attention there.

Some things get our attention straightaway; these seem to be innate, such as the smell of smoke or a loss of balance. Otherwise we have a fantastic capacity to simply delete what we sense. I (Joseph) rented a flat many years ago that was directly over a train station. I could have leaned out of the window and dropped paper onto the roofs of the trains underneath. The first few mornings I woke up with the first train at about half past five. After that, I slept through the noise. The new and different is what catches our attention. When it is no longer new, it just becomes 'the way things are'. Background music soon fades so far into the background we do not hear it. We delete sights as well as sounds. The wallpaper that appears garish when we move into a new place (and why is it that the person who decorated immediately before us always has the most appalling taste in furnishings?) soon becomes a familiar part of the house.

So, for example, when you meet a romantic partner, there will be small habits and ways of talking – the way she throws her head back when she laughs, the way he strokes his cheek when he is thinking – that are new and endearing. As you get to know each other, what was new becomes old, and what is old and familiar can become irritating. After a few years, those same habits that we find attractive in courtship can become annoying. A man may love the way a woman is spontaneous and charming in company when they first meet. A few years later, exactly the same behaviour can appear to him as naïve and embarrassing. A woman may love a man's energy in the first months and then start to wonder how she found such domineering behaviour attractive. The behaviour may not change, but our response may.

Alternatively, we may automatically filter out something unless our attention has been drawn to it. I (Robin) once worked for a company where the fleet of company cars was all deep brown in colour. I hated my car. The colour was revolting. As I drove along I was convinced everyone was turning to look at me to pass critical comments about the colour. What made matters worse was that I was convinced we were the only people who had such awful cars. Once in the car, however, I began to see deep brown cars everywhere. Each turning I took there would be a deep brown car coming my way. Up until then I had never noticed deep brown cars. I had filtered them out of my recognition.

The conditioned voice acts as a channel. It is both the result of paying attention to parts of our experience and also what causes us to be selective in what we observe. It is like a riverbed that is formed originally from small weaknesses and rivulets in the rock, but once it is formed, it channels the river that way and the flow of water only serves to make it deeper. But a river can form a new path and we can change parts of our conditioned voice.

If we believe the world is a rich and wonderful place, then we will tend to notice all the examples around us that support that belief. If we believe all members of the opposite sex are stupid, then that is what we will be on the look out for and therefore that is what we will notice. Our beliefs act as self-fulfilling prophecies.

We had a mutual friend some years ago whose self-esteem was about as low as it could fall. His father kept him out of trouble by making him so frightened he had no confidence to do anything without permission. His mother kept him under control by telling him he was worthless. As a result, this friend grew up believing that all women would bully him and make him feel bad about himself. So strong was this belief that it caused him to be attracted only to those women he knew *would* bully him and make him feel bad about himself. He spent years recovering from failed relationships saying, 'I told you so,' to his friends and himself to reinforce what a failure he was. He eventually married a woman who nagged him unremittingly. His parents despaired at his ineptitude in life. His family wanted him to do better, but unfortunately they always started their self-improvement lectures with the idea of how useless he was. The strongest message was that he was a failure. And we might guess that his wife may well have married him in the belief men are weak and do nothing without being nagged. When we form a couple our beliefs often dovetail like pieces of a jigsaw puzzle. The pieces may fit together to make a bright happy picture or a dull joyless picture, it all depends on the beliefs we begin with. We confirm ourselves in our weaknesses as much as in our strengths.

## MAKING SENSE OF IT ALL

Everything about relationships takes on meaning. A member of the opposite sex glances in our direction and smiles. Are they being friendly? Should we go over and start a conversation? Or are they smiling at our bad dress sense? If they are interested, we feel excited. If the smile was one of pity we may feel affronted or ashamed. So first we react to what happens. Then we act, maybe by starting a conversation or turning away and blushing.

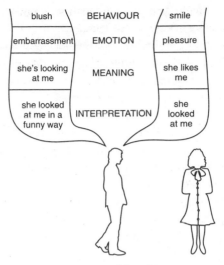

| blush | BEHAVIOUR | smile |
| embarrassment | EMOTION | pleasure |
| she's looking at me | MEANING | she likes me |
| she looked at me in a funny way | INTERPRETATION | she looked at me |

Streams of thought

We act from our interpretation, but this of course may not be right. One of the secrets of good relationships is to check your conclusions. In close relationships this is particularly important, for the closer the relationship, the more we care about what happens. A casual acquaintance can be rude and we will shrug it off. When our partner is rude, we may be hurt and wonder why they did it.

There are three ways to avoid misunderstandings, especially when someone hurts your feelings:

1  Trace your own reasoning in your own mind and question whether you have drawn reasonable conclusions from what you saw and heard.

2  Make your own reasoning clear. Say what you noticed and the conclusions you drew and how you feel about that if appropriate. Check whether the meaning you have taken is actually what the other person intended.

3  Check other people's reasoning. Ask them to describe how they came to their conclusions and see if there is any merit in their interpretation.

For example, I (Joseph) had an argument with my wife about some work around the house. I said I felt competent to do it. She said I was incompetent. I felt hurt and withdrew. She felt what she said was true and realistic. When we talked about it later, we discovered 'competent' meant two very different things to us. I thought I was competent if I felt I could do something, regardless of whether I had already done so in the past. 'Competence' for me is a feeling and a state of mind. I considered what my wife had said to be a judgement about myself. For my wife, competent simply meant you had succeeded in the past, it was a description only, not a judgement. Therefore, as I had not done this work before, I was automatically incompetent.

There are two dangers to avoid if you want to communicate clearly. One is to explain your own position too much and not bother with finding out what the other person thought. The second is an inquisition as to what the other person *really* meant (often hoping that eventually they will agree you were right in the first place).

We all think we know the right way to behave in relationships and we all think we know how a relationship should progress. Sometimes we even think we know others better than they know themselves – all based on our experience.

Wouldn't life be easier if when we met someone they handed us a list containing the messages that their internal voice sends them? Think of all the time we would save not having to discover through experience that their sense of what is important and true in relationships was different from ours? Very often, by the time we discover we do not see eye to eye it is too late, we are already committed emotionally. Then we try to change the other person or hope that they will change because of our love; we want them to see the world the way we do.

Our ability to notice someone's beliefs and values is important in relationships. Attraction usually starts on the physical level, but it needs to move above the genitals to the head if a resulting relationship is to be firmly grounded.

So, how can you uncover someone's values? Just listen to what they say and watch what they do. People demonstrate their sense of self, their beliefs and values, with every move that they make. When you are attracted to someone, instead of just feeling how turned on you are by their presence, start to notice how their life rules and view of the world are revealed in their behaviour.

## VOICE LEVELS

The conditioned voice whispers different sorts of information and keeps us updated on a number of different levels. We can subdivide our conditioned voice into separate categories. Each part can affect any other part. We will look at the parts individually first so that you can start to identify those messages that help you in relationships or those that get in the way. Later in the book we will cover ways to change those that limit you.

We will use the neurological levels developed by the American trainer Robert Dilts to clarify the different levels of the conditioned voice. These levels are a useful analytical tool and they are a good starting-point from which to see the levels of influence of the conditioned voice.

### Identity

The first level is identity. This is the level of our self-image – who we think we are. However, we have different self-images for the different environments or groups in which we operate. In the rock opera *Tommy*, written and performed by the group the Who, the main character was a deaf, dumb and blind boy who achieved very little in life until he played the pinball machine in the amusement arcade. Away from the pinball machine his self-image was one of misfortune, failure and isolation. When playing the pinball his self-image was as high as it could go, a complete contrast to how he normally 'saw' himself. What was his real identity? He made it for himself.

We all have our own self-image in relationships. It might be 'I'm a great catch', 'I am a true and honest lover', 'a cruel lover', 'a lady killer', 'a loser' or 'a heartbreaker', 'someone who is always there for you', 'homemaker', 'siren' or 'Don Juan'. Whatever the few words are that summarize your sense of self in relationships, they will influence your relationships profoundly.

I (Robin) have a friend, let's call him Steve, whose mother left home when he was very young. He was brought up by his father and in his early adolescence he made contact with his mother again after years of absence. His mother had remarried and had another son. My friend was introduced to his half brother who, by a strange coincidence, was also called Steve. It was only as she introduced them that it suddenly struck his mother that she had given both her sons the same name. Then she said to my friend, 'How silly of me. I forgot all about you.' Imagine how that must have affected his sense of self-worth. At that point he had a decision to make. He could accept that he was the sort of person who was so insignificant that his own mother could forget his name. He could decide that he was OK, but his mother was a dreadful, uncaring harridan. Or he could accept that he was OK and his mother was basically OK, but confused and had made an unthinking mistake. She could have his sympathy rather than his condemnation. The first two decisions tend to come more easily than the third. Unfortunately, we do not know which way he decided, but his upbringing and sense of self up to that point would have influenced his decision.

### SELF AND THE OTHER

Self-images can be negative, neutral or positive. Someone with a weak self-image may pick a 'trophy' partner, someone they pick not as a real person in their own right but someone who makes them look good.

Someone with an inflated sense of themselves, on the other hand, often appears arrogant. Some people see such a partner as a challenge. They will try to bring them down to earth or to prove their own power by changing them. The difficulty with this approach is that people with an inflated sense of self are the most difficult to change.

Are you looking for a partner or a vehicle for boosting your own self-esteem? Are you looking to prove your own power by dominating or capturing the most difficult of prey?

### PERSONALITY

Where does personality fit in? Interestingly, the word itself is an abstract noun which comes from the Greek word *persona*, which was the word used for a mask that was worn by an actor to disguise who they really were.

We may accuse people of 'not having much personality' yet we all think we have one of our own. How do we show our personality? Does it exist apart from what we actually do?

How would you describe your personality? Take a moment to make a description...
Now look at the words you have used. Can any of them exist in isolation? Maybe you have used words like 'caring', 'trustworthy' or 'creative', but whatever you have used, these descriptions must involve a relationship.

---

So, if your identity is the way you see and experience yourself, your self-image, the face you know behind the mask, then your personality is the way you function in a relationship with others. And just as with masks, you are free to choose a different one if you do not like the one you are wearing.

## Beliefs and Values

The next level within your conditioned voice is your beliefs and values – what you believe to be true about yourself and your relationships and what is important to you within your relationships. Beliefs cover statements such as: 'Marriage should be for life', 'You should start off as you mean to go on', 'If you're honest with them they'll be honest with you', 'One day I'll meet someone nice', 'Do it to them before they do it to you.' Sometimes we confuse beliefs with facts.

Values are what is important to you in relationships. They come out in statements like: 'It's important to be caring', 'I want someone who will love me', 'I wouldn't stay with someone who had an affair.' This is an important area that we will look at in greater detail later. Remember what you believe to be true and what is important to you are filters to the information you see, hear and feel. Your beliefs and values can be the gateway through which prospective partners can pass or obstacles that get in the way.

Some values make human society possible; others vary from culture to culture. For the peace lovers amongst us it is ludicrous to end human life for a cause. However some people have a view of reality that makes it possible for them to murder and slaughter in pursuit of a goal. Some of the gravest crimes in human experience have been carried out by people believing that what they were doing was correct. On the other hand, many suffer all manner of personal pain and hardship to help others, believing it is better for them to suffer than other people. In both cases, the more extreme the deed, the more unshakeable the faith in the righteousness of their action.

When I (Joseph) was 10 years old, I attended a rough school in west London. It was short of space, so our playground was on the roof. I do not remember how high the safety railings were, but the standard threat in this school was to intimidate someone by asking them if they wanted to 'take the dive' onto the tarmac below or ask them how they would like to 'smell the concrete'. I was a seven-stone weakling, consequently I relied on my wits for survival and joined the most fearsome gang of the school, because one of the members was the largest and toughest boy on the block. If someone gave me trouble, they would have to answer to him. One day I got into a fight with another member of the gang and knocked him over. That felt good at the time, but later I felt bad. The action felt good, but afterwards I did not like the feeling. Defending myself came naturally, but hurting someone else did not. I did not believe it was right to hit them and it seemed alien to my identity.

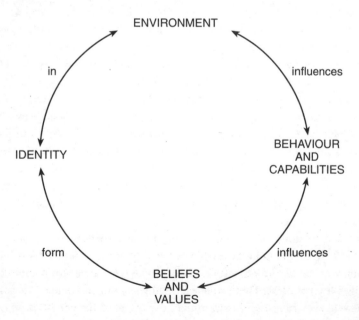

Neurological levels in a circle

## Skills and Actions

Your sense of self, your values and beliefs have a profound influence on the next level, which is your skills and actions – what you do and what you are capable of. Identity, beliefs and values act like an automatic pilot driving what we can achieve.

For instance, if you have a belief that members of the opposite sex cannot be trusted, then this will drive you towards people who can confirm through their untrustworthiness that your belief is valid. You will act with suspicion, seeing things that may not be there. And this will happen even if your common sense and intelligence tell you that you are being stupid in not trusting. Not to trust will seem like the right way to be and to be trusting would seem alien, uncomfortable and leave you feeling vulnerable. You may become expert at finding partners who will validate your belief. However, positive beliefs can leave you vulnerable to being exploited. The balance between trust and safety is a delicate one, which we shall cover in depth later.

## Environment

The final level is our environment – the place we are in and the people we are with. What sort of places do we favour? What sort of people do we like to be with?

Imagine someone who feels incomplete without a partner for life. Their beliefs and values around relationships might be that a trusting, monogamous, close and loving partnership is what works best. They will not look for a suitable partner in clubs renowned for attracting people seeking fleeting sexual relationships. We put ourselves in places with people that accord with our beliefs, values and sense of self or else we feel 'out of place'.

Your identity, beliefs, values and the internal voice that keeps you in touch with them are well established at an early age. Your environment, culture, family and education drip feed repeated information about how life is meant to be. There will be additions, subtractions and alterations throughout your life. However, the foundation to the conditioned voice seems to be pretty well formed before you can read.

Years ago my family and I (Robin) moved to a new house. Our new neighbours were a couple with two young daughters of the same age as my daughter. Wanting to be neighbourly, we invited the eldest child to come into our garden to play with our daughter. Her mother was convinced her daughter would not want to come across the fence. She said, 'She won't come. She won't leave her mum. She's a bit shy. She doesn't like strangers. Maybe when she knows you better she'll come and play.' Ignoring these protestations, I reached out to the girl, who held up her arms, and I lifted her over the fence to play. The child's mother was most upset that her daughter would leave her side. This charade of us offering to have the child to play and the mother's protestations that she was too shy went on for weeks. Eventually the child got the message and pretended to be too shy. Now she is grown and married. She lives four doors away from her mother and she visits every day. In fact, she still has her meals with her mother while her husband fends for himself. She has little contact with anyone else except for her children, all of whom are excellent at shyness.

The conditioned voice can also be shaped by one important experience. When I (Robin) was five, my father died. On the morning of his death my brother and I were sitting in the living-room with my mother and grandmother. We had yet to be told the bad news. There was a cold chill of foreboding in the room even though it was August. My mother and grandmother were looking at each other with uncertainty. I now suspect they were gathering courage. They told us the news. My world crumbled. Then my grandmother said, to pacify and to help me, full of the most positive of intent, wanting only to take my pain away, that I would have to be a big boy now and look after my mother. From that moment childhood left and I began to see out of adult eyes. My sense of self, my beliefs about my role in life and what I had to do were set as though a hypnotist had clicked their fingers and triggered them in an instant.

However, in the same way, the conditioned voice can also be changed in an instant. A sudden shock or confrontation can wipe the slate clean and put in place a new set of sense of self, belief and values.

A couple we knew were blissfully happy, living in perfect compatibility. The man existed for his work. He demanded his dinner when he got home, smoked his pipe, read novels in the bath and had the children presented to him before their bedtime so he could give them a goodnight kiss before he went down to the pub to have a few drinks with his friends. His wife had been raised by her grandmother and had inherited many of the beliefs held by that generation. She loved looking after her children, enjoyed the shopping, cooking, the cleaning and the washing. She saw herself as part servant and part lover. Her role was to make the home a comfortable place for her working husband to return to. She saw the lack of acknowledgement her husband gave her as being a positive sign that all was well and everything was going smoothly. Many of her friends thought she was unfulfilled, she seemed to get so little out of life. She was puzzled by their concern, for she had all that she had been brought up to expect.

For many years this dance of compatibility carried on between the two of them. Then the wife fell ill. She had a hysterectomy and there were complications. She lay at the point of death. The priest was called to give the last rites. Friends sat in the hospital corridors, silent and worried. She knew little about this time and did not realize that her husband was not at her side. Thankfully she recovered and people rallied round. Her husband visited with a bunch of flowers and a great show of affection. She went home and back to life as it was before her illness. Then a friend let slip that her husband had not been at her side when she was near to death. Full of pain, she asked him why he had not been there with her. He said he could not see what he could have done in the circumstances, with her being so ill, so he had stayed at work.

The next day he came home like a scolded dog with its tail between its legs. He had been thinking through how he had been during his wife's illness and had realized that if she had died life would have been awful. He said, word for word, 'If you'd have gone I'd have had to give up work to look after the children and I couldn't stand not working.' Narcissus could have learned something about self-absorption from this man.

The shock of her husband's selfishness changed this lady in an instant. It opened her eyes to what others saw. And she did not like it. She made no conscious decision at the time. However, the shock caused her self-image to change and this new sense of identity started to have an effect. It was as if her old image had been broken like a vase thrown against a wall. She lost her excess weight and started dressing smartly and sexily. She found herself a part-time job, met someone she liked who valued her for who she was in herself, not what she could do for him, and left her husband and family for a new life with her new man.

Six months before, her friends would have gambled their last pound on her being the last person in the world to walk out on her family.

Fortunately, everything turned out well. The husband remarried and the children were cared for and kept in contact with both parents.

Of course, these are only the highlights of this story based on what we heard and saw. There must have been other factors involved of which we were unaware. But it is an example of how a shock can reverse the sense of self, alter beliefs and values, and, in the wake of those changes, influence what you are capable of doing.

## PARENTS AND FAMILY

Our parents are the biggest contributors to our conditioned voice. Parental input comes in two forms. First, there is the information parents encourage and even force us to take on board. Secondly, there is information we choose to believe and copy. Some things we want to copy, others we only know we have copied when we are able to look back and compare.

This modelling may go very deep. I (Joseph) remember very clearly telling my daughter off when she was seven. I suddenly stopped and realized that what I had just said was exactly what my mother used to say to me in similar circumstances. I had repeated the phrase word for word and even used the same voice inflections. Underlying this must have been many of the values and beliefs about parents and children that I had inherited from my mother.

When we are young, we have only one model of how men and women behave towards each other, and how to raise children, and that comes from our parents. Because we are the product of those beliefs, values and ways of acting, sometimes it seems as if to question them is to question ourselves. Because of this, many of us find partners and situations that remind us of what our early home life was like. This is why some men and women end up with partners rather like their parents in appearance and attitude and why some couples replicate the love or conflict of their childhood.

I (Robin) attended a christening recently. The mother of the baby was in her mid-twenties. Her husband and father looked like identical twins. The scene was made even more incongruous because her husband called his father-in-law 'mister' and the father-in-law called his son-in-law 'lad'.

## The Best Possible

When we become adult we often focus more on what was wrong as opposed to what was right in the way that our parents brought us up. We see the narrowness and limitations of what they did. Given the knowledge they gathered in the process of bringing you up, your parents, too, would probably act differently given a second chance. But they did the best they could with the resources and knowledge available to them. That does not make everything all right. But the fact that you are questioning them is a sign that you can go outside the conditioning of your upbringing and evaluate from a more rational and mature perspective. It would be far worse to accept unthinkingly their ways as the best possible. It was probably the best possible that *they* could do, although with hindsight you can see it may not have been the best possible for you. Dealing with the idea may be difficult because parents are the objects of our deepest loves and our strongest hates at a time when these are strong and not easily controlled. Becoming mature is moving beyond our parents both physically and emotionally.

A psychotherapist friend of ours estimates that the vast majority of his clients' problems stem from poor parenting. He also recognizes that the mistakes have originated from the best of intentions. He jokes that he earns a living putting right all the 'good' that parents do. Many people feel their parents let them down – and so they did. And it is over. A greater tragedy would be to spend the rest of your life searching for a substitute parent that will give you all the things you felt you needed then but did not get.

The poet Philip Larkin summarized much of this ill feeling in his 1971 poem 'This Be the Verse':

They fuck you up, your mum and dad.
They may not mean to, but they do.
They fill you with the faults they had
And add some extra, just for you.

But they were fucked up in their turn
By fools in old-style hats and coats,
Who half the time were soppy-stern
And half at one another's throats.

Man hands on misery to man.
It deepens like a coastal shelf.
Get out as early as you can,
And don't have any kids yourself.

Philip Larkin puts the extreme view and if this were held by everyone, then the human race would soon be over.

The genetic voice encourages us to have children and children have to learn to be social. They do this in the only way they can – by copying the people around them. Children are wonderful at doing this and they are not very discriminating. Adults are bigger than they are. They are good at walking and talking, eating and drinking, and children assume that they are also good at doing everything else. They have made it into the magic land of adulthood where children want to go, where they can go to bed when they like and eat as much chocolate as they like. Children do not discriminate about the finer points of their parents' character. Age and size and availability are all the child looks for initially in a role model. As we grow, we become more discriminating, but the original modelling is the most enduring, because it is so basic. The younger we are, the more malleable and impressionable our character, like wet clay, yet we do have a character of our own from birth. As we grow older, so the clay dries and becomes less impressionable. Only later we decide who will impress us.

During those early formative years, however, our parents or those adults who care for us are the centre of our universe. They feed us, clothe us, wash us, love and nurture us. We try to please them so that they will keep looking after us. Imitation is the sincerest form of flattery, so is it any wonder that we decide to emulate our parents? And if these Godlike figures say that you are a stupid boy or girl, is there any wonder we take that information on board and build our sense of self-identity with it?

One of the ironies of modelling ourselves on our parents is that we rarely model the total package. Parents tend to fight in public and love in private. So if all we see is the public manifestation of their relationship we will tend to only copy that. Also, we model what they do more than what they say. This ability to read non-verbal signals is one of those rare skills that diminish with age. As we learn to talk, we place more importance on words, whereas when we are children we know that the real message is in the action and in what we hear in voice tone and inflection.

## Parental Immortality

Why do parents wish to impart beliefs and values, and shape the self-image of their children? Part of the reason is the desire for genetic immortality. Better than having a child inherit your genes, colouring and appearance is to have them inherit your beliefs and behaviour. If a parent sees their child become like them, it proves they are right to be the way they are. This is not a problem as long as the parent can deal with children who do not become like them. Parents need to give children permission to be themselves.

A man I (Robin) knew was proud of the lessons he had learnt from his strong and cynical father. When he was a child his father stood him on a high wall and told him to jump down, telling him that he would catch him. The child jumped. The father moved out of the way, allowing the child to fall to the ground and hurt himself. The lesson in this was that the child should never trust anybody in life, then he would not get hurt. The boy took this message on board and was really pleased to have learnt so early in life that people could not be trusted. He went through life never trusting, smug about the disappointments that this early experience had saved him from. When I asked him about not being able to trust his wife and the poor quality of the marriage that had resulted from his inherited beliefs, he said he would rather have had this sort of bad marriage than one in which he exposed himself emotionally and suffered pain. He went on to give his own children the same message, as full of positive intention as his own father had been, but he had an emotionally narrow life.

The important point is not to distrust unthinkingly, as this man did, or to trust blindly, which may be misplaced, but to be alert *in the moment* to the signals another person is giving you. Then *you* decide whether trusting them is right at the time.

Many parents feel that they have spent a lifetime learning the lessons of life and want to save their children the bother of the learning process. They see it as their duty to make sure their children understand the world the 'right way'.

However, despite the centuries-long efforts of philosophers, there has never been any agreement, let alone any guarantee of a right way. 'People spend a lifetime looking for the answer to life,' wrote the American writer Gertrude Stein. 'There is no answer. There never has been an answer. That's the answer.'

For all practical purposes, there are many right ways, because a right way is the one that works, the one that allows us to live our life in joy and fulfilment. Beliefs are our working hypotheses, like navigation charts for a ship. We use them as long as they take us on the course we want. Beliefs that lead us onto the rocks can be replaced, otherwise we will be like a ship's captain ploughing on regardless, thinking that the map is more real than the rocks they are aground on.

There is another reason parents want to shape their children. They had a dream when they started their family, a picture of what it would be like when their children grew into the people that they wanted to parent. They also knew from the start how they wanted their children to behave in public, with relatives and on different social occasions. That is why parents leap up and down with delight when their children start to walk and then shout at them to sit down when they run. It is why parents celebrate their children's first words and then tell them to be quiet when they say too much.

Some parents feel helpless when a child cries. A baby's cry has a keenness and directness that cuts through everything else. It demands to be answered. It jerks parents awake in the middle of the night when they have just slept through a jumbo jet accelerating overhead. It is natural to want to help. And sometimes they cannot and this is hard to bear. Parents who try to stop a child crying from their own sense of helplessness rather than the child's need may get angry with the child for making them feel bad. Allowing the natural expression of pain or grief is too painful for them. But if as a child you learn that it hurts your parents if you show emotion, how can you ever learn to show love?

One of the ways to make children presentable is to restrain their spirit and make them compliant. This way, to have the family of your dreams is to force them into a mould. This creates a nightmare. Evidence suggests that the more we try to force children to go against their natural selves, the more resistant they are, and the more likely we will be to pay the wages of psychotherapists, social workers and psychiatrists in later years.

Parental expectations of children can apply enormous pressure. Some parents may even see their children as possessions and feel free to do with them what they want. If parents see their children as a means of correcting their own mistakes, fulfilling their dreams by proxy, becoming the people they wish they themselves have been, it will cause conflict within the children. They will want to both please their parents and be true to themselves and their own identity. Very often these two outcomes are mutually exclusive and conflict arises.

When I (Robin) was a boy, I was friendly with the son of the local chemist. This chemist had wanted very much to become a doctor, but had failed. He forced his son to study almost every hour of the day in order to be the doctor he had never been. The lad looked grey and drawn, and never played with the rest of us. I never saw him smile. I have often wondered if he made the grade and made his father happy. I wonder if he ever had the chance to choose freely what he wanted to do with his life.

Beliefs, values, sense of identity, the family attitude to life and the world view are passed from one generation to the next as you would pass down heirlooms. In the past, trades were built on the cascading down of the conditioned internal voice. The sons of blacksmiths, for example, were brought up to believe that being a blacksmith was their destiny, it was in their blood. To please their fathers and receive attention in return, they would spend time in the forge. There they would learn what a worthwhile and valuable function it was. They would feel motivated to learn the skills, be happy with the behaviour involved in the process and the environment in which they would work. On a national level this form of apprenticeship created a wealth of skills. On the family level it worked also, because it guaranteed the trade would continue to provide income. The same principles still apply to relationships. And not all people want to be hammering at their close relationships like blacksmiths.

## Parental Input and the Conditioned Voice

What influence does parental input have on our conditioned voice and the relationships we form? It may be very positive. If we have been brought up to feel good about ourselves and have developed a strong and confident self-image we will probably be able to handle relationships easily. If our parents have demonstrated love towards each other in front of us then we will have a worthwhile model to emulate. If they have encouraged, through demonstration and discussion, a set of beliefs and values that focus on doing what is best for us without harming or using others, then we will probably make our partners as happy as we are. If we have been directed by information and positive encouragement to make our own decisions about what is right and wrong for us and others, we are likely to be well balanced and capable of dealing with whatever life puts before us. Our life experience will also let us re-evaluate these parental messages.

I (Robin) know that my mother was born into a working-class family where everyone knew their place. My grandfather was quite certain that there were those born to be rich and those born to work. We were meant to be poor. Know your place was the order of the day. When we were 11, my brother and I both qualified for grammar school, a form of secondary school education for those who demonstrated they were academically in the top 10 per cent of students. During my first week at this school I overheard other boys talking about something called university. They were all, apparently, working in order to go there. When I went home that evening, I asked my mother what university was. She told me university was not for people like us. She meant no harm. She was speaking the truth according to her view of the world, the one she had inherited from her father. From that moment on I stopped working at school. From being a very bright boy I became one of those that made up the numbers. My mother's comment had so shaped my sense of self that I believed I was born to live a limited life. Those limitations stayed with me for many years. I became quite expert at failure. It was not until I started a successful career in sales that I was able to allow my intellect to step in and challenge my negative self-image. Once I had discovered that there were no limitations to what I could achieve – unless I wanted there to be a limitation – I started to study and learn.

## HOME ASSOCIATIONS

For most of us, our first home with our parents is associated with happiness, love and safety. Whatever the reality, in our child's view it is the only description of love and safety that we have. We are born with an expectation of being looked after and loved. Therefore anything that reminds us of home will trigger in us that same sense of love, safety and happiness.

How does this work? Think back to a piece of music that was played at an earlier time in your life. Play that music in your head. Do you notice your mood change? Do you experience feelings now that you had back then? Now think of a smell from a time past that is very evocative and imagine that smell again. Did that change your mood and take you back to how you felt then? Do the same with a picture or a taste of something you used to touch. Better still, trigger these senses with the real experience. Play an old record or smell some old scent, pick up a childhood toy. Memories are held within our five senses. Reconnection to those memories through our five senses will trigger the emotional response we had at the time. That is why we can be tempted to re-create the past in order to re-experience those emotions of happiness, love and safety.

So we are often attracted to people who would have fitted in well in the home of our upbringing. Boys are often attracted to women similar to their memory of their mothers in appearance and behaviour. It is why you might choose a relationship that is no better than your parents' relationship because it is familiar. You might choose someone you think you can turn into one of your parents. Children have a keen sense of justice. They want things to be right. If they are not, they may grow into an adult who spends the rest of their life creating dysfunctional relationships in order to try to mend those hurts in the past.

This desire to reconstruct the past also explains why sometimes, if our parents hurt us, we will find a partner who will hurt us too. It is why if our parents needed rescuing we might find a partner who needs rescuing. It also explains why some people seem to end up with the most unexciting and drab of partners after a sequence of attractive and fun ones – the fun ones do not reconstruct the past. If home meant conflict, then our conditioned voice will need conflict in order for us to experience love, safety and happiness that we thought we had during our upbringing. This phenomenon of meeting someone who would have fitted in well at home is one explanation for love at first sight. The response is not so much attraction as familiarity.

However, if our memories of childhood are poor and the models of relationship that influenced us are negative, there is always the chance that we will rebel and be completely different. In a gesture of independence and rejection we will be everything our parents did not want us to be. We might even choose a partner because we know our parents would hate them. When this happens, we are just as much under parental control as if we were obeying. Whether we rebel or comply, if we only react without choice then we are not being true to ourselves.

---

Try this experiment.

Make a list of all the words that you associate with home. These will be your anchors to love, safety and happiness.

You can then turn these words into short sentences. For instance, one of the words on my list is 'food', therefore my sentence is 'Home means food.'

If you then repeat your list, substituting the words 'love, happiness and safety' for 'home', you end up with sentences such as 'Love, happiness and safety mean food.' How does this fit in with your life and how you approach relationships?

If some of the words on your list are negative, such as 'violence', 'pain', 'hurt' or 'punishment', then your sentences may make some interesting reading. This exercise may throw some light onto what you are re-creating in your life. For instance, for one client, 'home' meant 'cold'. Therefore 'love, happiness and safety' meant 'cold'. It was no surprise that his wife found it difficult to give and receive affection.

---

## FAMILY AND FRIENDS

Belonging to a group outside the family is a major step to independence. Groups are usually formed based on shared beliefs and values. Those wishing to join will feel pressured into matching those beliefs and values in order to gain acceptance and therefore not be left on their own. Consequently, if your group has certain attitudes towards relationships, you will feel compelled to match those views.

With siblings or groups there is invariably a pecking order which is often based on age and size. To maintain dominance, older siblings or friends will intimidate the younger ones into compliance. This often involves reducing the younger one's self-image and sense of identity. This self-image can remain for the rest of their lives.

As group views often emanate from the strongest personality or leader of the group and as those attitudes are often handed down from their parents, we also start to pick up other attitudes to supplement those we already have from our parents. These new attitudes may be positive. However, the desire to fit in can often need you to accept and demonstrate values and beliefs that conflict with those you already hold. The greater the number of people who hold a view, the more you are likely to comply.

For example, I (Joseph) started smoking when I went to university. Before this I disliked the idea and hated the smell. My parents encouraged me not to smoke by saying they would give me money if I did not smoke before my twenty-first birthday (presumably on the grounds that if I made it to 21 without smoking I would probably be safe for the rest of my life). Thinking back, however, there was another message in their offer – smoking was so attractive that I had to be bribed not to do it. At college, all my friends smoked and shared cigarettes as a way of being friendly and being part of the group. The social pressure allied with the ambiguity of my parents' message (my mother smoked) was too much and I became a smoker.

Social pressure can also affect our views on relationships. Much of our society is structured to suit couples. There is often a subtly expressed expectation on us all to pair up. 'Still on your own, darling?' is a much-used expression of interest received as criticism. Many people feel they are letting their parents down by not living a 'normal' family life. Certain professions such as politics almost demand the right family image for promotion and progression. Often our fear of being on our own has more to do with what other people think than with what we want to do with our lives. Forming a relationship to shield yourself from parental or social pressure will, however, rarely bring complete happiness. There is a case to be made for having nobody instead of the wrong body. With nobody you may be moderately unhappy. With the wrong body you might be totally miserable.

## EDUCATION

The word 'education' comes from a root that means to 'draw out'. Education starts from the idea of developing your mind. Unfortunately, the meaning seems to have been reversed, so that now it means putting in. Say 'education' and what is likely to immediately come into your mind is pictures and sounds of schools. However, education does not mean school. English law recognizes this, for it states that a child must have an education but does not have to go to school to get it.

Nearly all of us will, however, have been to school. What comes into your mind when you think of your school? How do you feel about it? What did it try to teach you? And what did you learn? At school we learn much more than the academic subjects that form the curriculum – we learn social skills, a view of the world; we see how our classmates make relationships; we often taken on beliefs about ourselves and our capabilities from our teachers. In some ways schools are like parents – they do their best, but when we look back we usually see all the things that could have been better.

Schools also teach us about relationships. Here is where we first try our social skills, make friends and enemies. This is where we see the opposite sex at close quarters. Apart from our parents, school probably has the greatest effect on the way we form relationships.

Some schools, especially many public schools in Great Britain, see as part of their function the installation of a sense of superiority and privilege in their pupils. Consequently, from the time they start attending school, children are inundated with words and actions that reinforce their superiority. These children grow up with an enhanced sense of identity and a belief in their own success. They form a sense of self that says they deserve the best, more than others do, and they will achieve anything they wish in life. With such a sense of self it is more likely that these children will succeed, consequently the whole process becomes a self-fulfilling prophecy.

If your criterion for success is achievement, then this method of education is an excellent model. If your criterion is good relationships, then you may need to think again. Feeling superior to a partner is dangerous unless your partner has a desire to maintain an inferior self-image.

Some teachers control by stimulation, engagement and making their subjects interesting and inspiring. Others control by reducing pupil self-esteem through ridicule and fear. This does work for the teachers in that it makes many students compliant, but if you have a poor self-image it is more difficult to form a rewarding relationship with others.

## THE MEDIA

Many children spend as much time watching television as they do at school. In days before television, the average exposure to drama was limited to the radio and a visit to the cinema or theatre. Now many of us sit beneath an avalanche of fictional portrayals of 'real life'. Television reflects real life and also influences it. To be interesting, drama has to be larger than life to catch the audience and these exaggerated dramas influence what we expect and how we act.

Advertising takes many of the biologically identifiable differences we looked at earlier and makes caricatures of them. Women become silly housewives who become orgasmic over clean washing. They live in little worlds without aspiration. Men are covered in grease and have spanners sticking out of their overall pockets. They pop to the pub while their wives fix the meal. All of these images must act as a backcloth, a slow and regular conditioning. If they did not work, advertisers would not use them.

Children's books, fairy tales, all add pieces to the jigsaw of the sense of self and beliefs and values. Many still expect the highlight of a girl's life to be when she walks down the aisle in her flowing white dress with her Prince Charming in waiting. Some parents dream of being able to give their daughters such a day. Walt Disney films have brought these dream images to countless numbers.

Because conflict works in drama, romantic love works in fairy tales and stereotypes work in advertising, this does not give them any relevance to real life. But they all affect our conditioned voice and the relationships we form.

## KNOW YOUR OWN VOICE

Why is it important to know and understand our conditioned voice? It's always been there and it sounds familiar, so why not just accept it as background noise that takes us wherever it wants? The reason it is important to know your conditioned voice is that then you can understand which messages work for you and which do not, which help you get what you want in life and which hinder you. The conditioned voice is like a hypnotist whispering in your ear and just like people who have been hypnotized, we may find ourselves carrying out orders while rationalizing about why we are doing so.

Hypnotic conditioning

In India, they have a way of training elephants. The young ones are taken from their mother and one of their legs is tied to a stake in the ground. The baby elephant struggles against the tether, but does not have the strength to break free. After a while it gives up. It does not try to break free again. It 'knows' that it does not have the strength, even when it has grown to four times the size. So the adult elephant can still be tethered and held by a thin rope around its foot, even though it could rip out the stake easily. It has given up trying. It 'knows' it cannot break free. Sometimes our conditioned voice tethers us in the same way.

Some behaviour that you demonstrate, inherited from generations back, will seem to an outside observer to have no purpose. The original belief or value that created the behaviour may have been lost in the mists of time. I (Robin) remember an occasion when my wife and children stood in the hall and watched me gather up all the rubbish, every last scrap of it, and put it out for collection. They never normally watch because the children are usually at school when I go through my rubbish ritual. They were mesmerized by my efficiency and thoroughness. So intent was I about my weekly chore that I never noticed them watching me. It was only when the job was finished and my family applauded that I took note. I had been so absorbed in what I was doing that it took an outside perspective to make me aware of it. I was treating the disposal of rubbish as though it were a matter of life or death.

When it comes to rubbish I copy my mother's behaviour in every detail. I had never questioned this up to that point, or even thought about my own attitude. As a boy I had watched my mother look out for the dustcart coming round the corner and observed her state of panic as she rushed about gathering every last piece of paper for disposal. That, to my young eye, became the way rubbish was taken out – full of panic, as though it was a matter of the gravest importance. It might be that my mother was herself simply mimicking her parents' behaviour. The reason for it may have been lost generations back. Maybe it goes so far back that it was originally to prevent the spread of disease during the Great Plague of London!

Likewise I was 26 before I realized you could get on a train without it being in motion. I had suspected it was possible, but my conditioning had always made me so late that I always had to get on with the train already making its way down the tracks. When I was a child, my mother would need to dress and organize three children and their luggage for a journey and she never left sufficient time. We would reach the station with the whistle blowing for departure and my mother would be pulling us along, opening a carriage door that flapped with the motion of the train. She would throw us on, followed by our luggage, and make a final leap herself like a rugby player making a last ditch tackle. Now I can organize myself well enough in advance to arrive at stations with time to spare. However, those same feelings of anxiety still fill me and a sense of relief still floods over me as I board.

These examples of inherited behaviour driven by inherited beliefs make little impact on my life. If anything, they create a little humour. What I found strange was how normal that behaviour felt, even though I had never rationally decided to adopt it. If I can be blind to the beliefs and behaviour I hold about such trivial matters, then I assume that I must also have hidden beliefs and behaviour around relationships.

I have, however, identified many of the beliefs I hold about women and how I relate to them. Many of them serve me well. Others once stood in the way and made life very unpleasant for the women whom wanted to get close to me. For instance, I learned to believe there was only one person in the world who was perfect for me. Not only were they perfect, they were also waiting for our paths to cross and then for happiness to settle upon us like blossom falling from trees. Intellectually I knew that there could not be just one person perfectly made for me and during those early days of high hormone activity my genetic voice was constantly telling me how gorgeous all girls were. However, always in the background, softly beguiling, yet loud enough to have an influence, was the voice that kept me looking for this special person. This message made me search for perfection. It caused me to be blind to the qualities of many of the girls I met because they did not fit the description my conditioned voice had manufactured.

We both knew a man who worked as an interior designer. His sense of self was dominated by his job. Indeed, his job was born out of his sense of self. If you asked him what he was like as a person he would answer that he was an interior designer. He had developed a self-image that involved creativity and enhancement. He believed everything could be improved. No matter how stunning the décor of a house he could find a way to make it better. It was important to him to be able to express his artistic capability in improving his surroundings.

He struggled with his romantic relationships, even though he found it relatively easy to date. He was good looking, wealthy, articulate, liked to spend money and go to interesting places. Unfortunately he could not understand his companions' resistance to being changed. He could not understand why they became annoyed when he tried to make them better. He had a picture in his head of how life and a partner should be and he unknowingly always chose somebody who would need to adapt to match his picture. For him to have found someone who fitted without alteration would have denied the need for the creative self that was part of his identity.

A sexual and romantic relationship is too important to leave to chance; you are choosing a person who will be closer to you than anyone else in the world. Every day you spend with them is your choice. They can bring you heaven or hell, depending how well you get on. It is surprising how many people not only do not give close relationships any serious thought, but even think that it is somehow not right to do so. And this leads to a lot of problems. Many people adopt a 'try it and see' approach to finding a partner. They date a number of people to see what works and what does not work. Although they are searching for compatibility, they may not know what compatibility would look like, feel like or sound like if it arrived. So they find themselves committed just by having spent time with someone. As the days or weeks of non-evaluation tick by, they may be too far in to get out again without the pain of break up, or they might settle for an unsatisfactory compromise, someone who is 'OK' but not really what they were looking for, although they were not sure what they were looking for in the first place.

Another common mistake is to look for someone we can change or mould into our ideal. In other words a person may realize that their ideal partner may not exist naturally, or that if they do then they may never meet them, but the ideal still holds their attention. They want it and not a real person. So they form a relationship with someone whom they sense they can change into their ideal.

This is like going into a shop and buying an outfit that you do not want, on the grounds that you can take it home, alter it and dye it a different colour! Of course it makes much more sense to buy an outfit you like in the first place, but you have to realize that there is more than one outfit that you can be happy with. People usually strongly resist being changed into something they are not, to please a partner. The message they get is that they are not OK in themselves. Also, because it is the ideal image that drives the relationship, the person will never be satisfied because ideals are, by definition, unobtainable. Both partners are likely to become disillusioned and frustrated over time, one because the other does not conform to the ideal and the other because they sense they are not valued for who they are, but for who they are not.

---

Take a moment to think who would be your ideal partner.

What would they look like?
What sort of voice would they have?
How would you feel about them?
How would they act towards you?
How would you act towards them?
Are you using anyone as a model for your ideal partner?

---

Ideals are *our* own creation. We can control every part of our ideal down to the last detail. We cannot control other people and make them what they are not, except for a very short time, and the price both of you pay is very high.

A man we know works as a lorry driver and he challenged us to explain something that puzzled him. One day after a long drive he had parked for a rest in an isolated area on the Yorkshire Moors miles from any habitation. On the other side of the car park was a small van next to an emergency telephone box. He was about to go to sleep when he noticed in the dim light that there were two people in the telephone box who seemed to be fighting. Being tired, he decided to let them get on with what they were doing and he locked his doors. Then, looking more carefully, he saw that one of the people was a woman and the other a man. The man appeared to be beating the woman. Not being a brave man, the truck driver thought about driving off, but his conscience would not let him. Grabbing a large spanner from his toolbox, he edged his way across the car park, pulled open the telephone box door and demanded that the man stop beating the woman. The bullying man was big, bull-faced and aggressive and he was snorting and salivating with anger. But to the truck driver's surprise it was the woman he had come to save who shouted abuse at his intrusion. She told him to mind his own business and go away, which he did, and the beating continued.

The truck driver asked how anyone could explain what had happened. Only the people in the telephone box could really explain their actions, but we imagine that those people needed to beat and to be beaten. It somehow made sense to them, made them feel that this was how life was supposed to be. Possibly they had both come from homes where a man beat a woman and what they were doing was what they thought everybody wanted to do. People look for what they want in a partner.

For most people the coming together in the dance of the conditioned voices is less traumatic. The person who likes to care will be attracted to someone who needs to be cared for. We form relationships with those whose view of the world complements ours.

When a person is dominated by their conditioned voice, then they may feel forced to seek a relationship that is just like the one they modelled from their parents. Alternatively, they may feel forced to seek what they did not get from their parents. The tragedy in this case is that they often pick someone just like their parent, who is incapable of giving them what they need, and so history repeats itself. In either case they will have difficulties with relationships.

## UNDERSTANDING OUR CONDITIONED VOICE

Now we are in a good position to explore the levels of our own conditioned voice.

### Environmental

First the environment level.

---

What environment did you grow up in?
What influence do you think this has on how you form relationships?

Now list the people with whom you have relationships, where you might go to meet people if you are unattached, where you go with a partner if you are in a relationship, the frequency of meetings and what happens while you are together.

Think about either finding a partner or building a relationship with a partner.

Where do you like to go?
Who do you like to go with?
What times do you like to go?
How do these choices open up or limit the sort of people you meet?
What aspects of your relationship do these places and people build?

---

One friend of mine took all his girlfriends down the pub. He had a wonderful time there with his mates, but most of his girlfriends did not and he broke up with them. Eventually he found a girl who enjoyed those times as much as he did.

If you are looking for a partner or have had difficulties finding the right partner, it might be interesting for you to notice where you go to meet people and how those places match your beliefs and values. Many people want to meet trusting partners for a long-term relationship, yet they go to places normally frequented by people looking for short-term contact with anybody who is warm and breathing.

## Behaviour and Capability

We are not going to prescribe any miracle remedies here, like 'Ten guaranteed tips to meet the partner of your dreams' (there is only one guaranteed way to meet the partner of your dreams and that is to go to sleep). There is something rather strange about these sorts of books – they seem to take away the other person's choice. Of course the answer is that there is no guaranteed way to attract the right partner and to have satisfying relationships, and any book that prescribes behaviour is going for the wrong level. Also, someone who puts a lot of effort into attracting the opposite sex is not always very attractive to the opposite sex. A relationship, if it is satisfying, will claim as much of you as you are willing to give. Prescribed behaviour will only take you a very small way.

Men and woman are just not predictable, even in everyday matters, and certainly not in how they love and whom they are attracted to. Anything you can do to explore *your* own ways of acting will help you to bring more to a relationship, so you are both attracting and attractive. We can control our own thoughts and actions to some extent. We cannot control other people. You enter a romantic relationship as a complete person. The way to satisfying relationships is to know yourself and know what works between you and another. Not every relationship can be perfect, but most can be better.

---

What kinds of things do you do when you are with your partner?
What activities do you share?
What do you both enjoy doing?
Are you limiting your sex life to any particular times and places?

Our conditioned voice has some very strong messages about sex, for example the times and the places where you can have sex and the kinds of sex you can have. So it often demands that the only right time and place for sex is at night in the bedroom. If you feel constrained by these sorts of messages, then fantasize for a moment what it would be like to have sex in other places and in other ways that attract you.

Notice what sort of objections come up for you. Notice which ones might have come from your family conditions. These are the ones you may want to think and explore a little more, perhaps talking over with your partner. No one should feel they have to engage in any sexual behaviour that they are not comfortable about, but if you feel limited for no good reason that you can understand, this may be your conditioned voice talking.

Now think of all the qualities you have in a relationship.
Make a list of all those things starting with: 'I can...' For example:

'I can make other people laugh.'
'I can make love in a satisfying way.'
'I can assess people's character quickly.'
'I can see the other person's point of view (even if I do not agree with it).'

A good way to do this is to think of what your partner has complimented you for doing. These are the things that matter to them. You may think very little of them, but they mean a lot.

Now make a list of those qualities that you would like to improve and any qualities that you would like to have. Would you like to be more assertive or caring or demonstrative? Add the reason you would like these qualities.

'I would like to be ... because...'

---

## Beliefs

Now to beliefs. Beliefs are our working rules; perhaps the best definition is: 'Beliefs are those ideas we accept despite evidence to the contrary.' We have beliefs about ourselves, about what is possible, about what we can do and about what we deserve. Remember that beliefs are not necessarily true, they are our best guess about how the world is based on our experience to date.

Many of our beliefs we take from the way our parents worked together as a couple. We see how they behave and we generalize. For example, when I (Joseph) was growing up, my father went out to work while my mother did all the household tasks. She also kept all the financial accounts for my father, who was self-employed. This was my only model when I was young. Now, of course social change has turned these beliefs and values upside-down, but I still sometimes catch myself feeling that this is the way that things really should be. Sometimes I get the sneaking feeling that I am doing my wife a favour when I do the household chores, that really it's her job. I do not think I am the only man in the world who feels this way either. Many men were brought up in households where the division of labour between their parents was the same as in my parents' home. Even the language in which we think about it can be ambiguous. Many men talk about 'helping' their wives with the housework, as though it is a favour, something that is not really their responsibility. Better to help than do nothing, however. Whatever arrangement you come to, make sure it works for both of you. Until we get smart houses that clean themselves, there will always be work to do that neither partner can get very excited about. It is easy to criticize and judge your parents' arrangements with the wisdom of hindsight. Yet your parents were doing the best they could in the times and social mores in which they lived. This does not make them wrong, but it does not make them right either.

It is well worth exploring what beliefs you may have picked up and still be hanging on to, despite evidence to the contrary. Try the following exercise.

---

What messages about how couples relate did you get from your father?
What messages about how couples relate did you get from your mother?
If you had any brothers and sisters, what messages about how couples relate did you get from them?
What messages about how couples relate did you get from your grandparents? (Your grandparents will probably show your parents' patterns, but even more so.)
What messages did you get from your peer groups about how couples relate?
Which of these attitudes and beliefs do you still hold?
Do you agree with them intellectually?

When you think of these questions, think about what your parents actually did, as well as what they told you. There were many tasks (like ironing) that my mother hated and said that she should not have to do, but she still did them. The action is stronger and makes more impression than the words.

Parental patterns may be completely inadequate in preparing you for life. The most important point is to see them for what they are: *your parents'* patterns, *their* answer to their society and the relationship they had, and to evaluate them for yourself rather than unthinkingly accepting or rejecting them.

Make a list of beliefs you have about relationships, all the things you believe to be true about yourself, yourself in relationships, your parents and to relationships in general. You might list statements such as 'I believe it is natural to form a lifelong association' or 'To make relationships work you need to work at them' or 'If you are open with a partner they will be open with you.' On the other hand you might believe that 'All members of the opposite sex are not to be trusted' or 'My status as a lover depends on the number of partners I have' or 'All's fair in love and war.'

Take some time over this list. You can add to it when a thought strikes you. Dig deep and remember to identify what you genuinely believe to be true and not what you wish were true.

What we *believe* we deserve may affect how we enter relationships. What sort of relationships do you think you deserve? And why?
Explore your beliefs by filling in the blanks of the following question. Be sensitive to your feelings as you think about it.

'I deserve relationships that are ... because...'

We all have beliefs about what we deserve based on our ideas about others and ourselves. Write what immediately comes into your mind and then consider it carefully:

Do you really feel that you deserve that?
If you have limited what you deserve in any way, what influenced you to do that?
Are any of these influences based on your experience and tested in real relationships?
Do you need to have a belief on the lines of, 'The sort of relationships I have will not change, but will always be the same as what happened in the past?'
If you do, how do you know that?

Here is a way you can explore any beliefs that might be limiting you in relationships.

First, think of the sort of really satisfying relationship you really want.
Then think what stops you from achieving what you want. Write down what comes to mind, even if it seems strange or silly.
What sort of objections are there? How many of these objections are real constraints of your environment and how many are your beliefs?
Now think what might be positive about that belief that seems to be stopping you achieving what you want. For example, it might be it keeps you from being rejected.
Then ask yourself, 'What would I rather believe?'
If you had the choice, what would you rather believe about yourself or others that would keep the same positive aspect, but let you be freer to get what you want in relationships?
Now think how your life would be different if you were to act as if that belief were true rather than the limiting one. Imagine a typical day in your life where that belief was true.

How satisfying would that be?
What would you be thinking?
What would you be doing?
Where would you be going?
How would you feel?
What sorts of things would you be saying?
How would your partner be responding to you?

---

When you think about it, the only thing that makes a limiting belief true is the fact that you act all the time as if it were true. Having a different belief won't change the world or your circumstances immediately, but it will goad you into action that will provoke changes of the sort you want. How do you know when someone believes something? You see how they act. To stop believing, you stop acting as if the belief were true. Act differently. Only then will you be able to really judge how true it might be.

A limiting belief can never be proved 'true' because you cannot prove a negative. For example, if you believe you cannot meet a partner who is kind and understanding and respects you, it does not mean they do not exist. You may have a series of bad relationships, but that does not prove that a good one is impossible, it means only that it has not happened yet. You cannot prove something does not exist, only that it does exist – when you find it. Beliefs about relationships are different from beliefs about the physical world. Gravity does not require your belief in it before it causes you to fall over. However, we often form our beliefs about ourselves, other people and relationships *as if* they were as immutable and unchanging as gravity.

Having positive beliefs is not unthinking Pollyanna-like optimism – you actually do not know what is true about other people. All you can say is that your beliefs affect your expectations, which affect your actions, which affect your experience. Therefore it makes sense to use beliefs that can help you and open doors rather than assume the doors are shut. Perhaps we are talking about acting on realistic hope.

One way we form beliefs is to generalize from one experience. We see a repeated pattern and think that things will always be like this. This is like flipping a coin, having it come up heads three times in a row and then believing that coins always come up heads and always will. Three heads in a row is quite possible and not particularly improbable.

I (Joseph) remember my daughter asking me a strange question when she was four years old. 'Daddy,' she said, 'will I have to break a bone to be grown up?'

I said, 'No, you won't. Why do you think you would have to?'

She told me that it seemed that every adult she had met had broken an arm when they were young. Only a few days earlier I had told her about the time when I fell in the garden and broke my wrist when I was 14. Thinking back, several other adults she knew had also told her that they had broken a bone when they were young. It is fairly common, certainly, but not compulsory! She had made the generalization that perhaps everyone had to and then got scared that she would have to as well. I am glad she decided to check with me first.

When we generalize, we generate a number of rules for ourselves about how the world is and what we must, must not, should and shouldn't do. We also have beliefs about what we can and cannot do.

Look over your list of beliefs about relationships and see if some of them include words such as 'have to', 'must', 'mustn't', 'can' and 'can't'. These will come from generalized beliefs that you hold about yourself in relationships, about relationships in general and about sexual partners.

For instance if you had said, 'I can't think of what to say when I am on a date,' that is a generalized statement drawn from your experience of the world and your conditioning. Also, of course, it is not true. You are perfectly capable of thinking what to say – although you might apply unrealistic criteria about how witty the remarks need to be. Nothing physical stops you. The mental barrier is what prevents you.

When you identify these sorts of beliefs, replace 'I can't' with 'I shouldn't' and see what sort of change this makes. So our previous example becomes: 'I shouldn't say anything when I am on a date.' Often this change can make your belief sound really funny. Now you can ask yourself a couple of questions. The first is: 'Who says?' Here is where you may catch a whisper of your parent's voice in your ear. The other question is: 'What stops me?' Nothing physical, clearly. It must be some imagined consequence or maybe a bad experience in the past that you are determined not to repeat.

Sometimes we learn the wrong thing from experience. We learn never to have that painful experience again, but that was a unique combination of people and circumstances. You could never have that experience again because time does not run backwards. The only way you can have that pain again is if you continually go over it in your mind and relive it. You could never exactly reproduce that experience anyway, you are older, you know more, you have seen more of life, the other people will be different, in different circumstances, etc.

---

When you find the sort of beliefs that start with, 'I can't...' or 'I shouldn't...', experiment with the tonality that you say them with.

Listen to yourself saying these sentences.
What sort of tonality does your voice have?
Whose voice is it?

You will usually find the belief comes over as a statement, for example, 'I shouldn't do that.' Try it with an incredulous voice tone rising at the end – 'I shouldn't do that?' It will not have the same power over you.

---

A limiting belief about making conversation implies that something dire would happen if you did. What might this be? Your answer might be that you would be rejected. If we then pursued this line of questioning and asked for the consequences of being rejected, you might then, after thought, conclude that you would have to walk away and start again. The consequences usually appear less dire once they have been given a description.

There is often a mental movie playing in your imagination that vividly illustrates the danger you want to avoid. For example, let's follow the belief 'I can't think of anything to say on a date.' What stops you? 'Everything I say will be uninteresting.' What would happen if you did? This is where there may be a mental movie of your partner laughing uncontrollably at your gauche remarks, finger pointing at you, convulsed with mirth – obviously a painful picture, but one that is *yours* and, like many of the mental movies of imagined consequences, rather over the top. Or you may imagine your partner saying to themselves that you are stupid and boring. This is also painful, but it is still mind reading – mind reading something that has not happened!

You may also have some beliefs that are about what you should or must do, for example: 'I must pay for my partner's meal' or 'I must always give in at the end of an argument.' Again, you might ask the same kind of questions: 'Who says?' and 'What would happen if you did not?' You can also change the tonality to one of incredulity: 'I must *always* give in at the end of an *argument*?'

These sorts of beliefs are usually held together by one or a few bad experiences in the past and your conditioned voice is not giving you the chance to make a proper test. When you look at these beliefs more critically, you will find they are not as substantial as they appear.

The other way beliefs show themselves is as statements that seem to be always true, no exceptions, for example, 'No one would ever fall in love with me.' These are very limiting. So are beliefs like 'Everyone seems to be happier in their relationships than me' or 'My partner never listens to me.' When you find a belief like this, put it into the past tense, because actually that is where it belongs. Preface each one with 'Up to now my experience has been...' Can you feel the difference that makes?

Also, these sort of generalized beliefs set you up to miss the times when they are not true. There is something satisfying in being proved right, even when the experience is a painful one. You can say, 'There, I told you so!' Also, we hold beliefs dear – some of them are almost part of our identity, part of the way we define ourselves. We talk about having beliefs, cherishing them, holding them, losing them, as if they were important possessions. So they are, in a way.

To challenge your limiting beliefs, try this exercise. If you can work with a friend or an understanding partner, then all the better.

---

Go back over your list of beliefs and identify any that include or imply words meaning 'never', 'always', 'without fail', 'all' and 'every'.

Then really search for any examples where this was not so. Has it been your consistent experience in every case? If there was even one time when it was not, then this belief is not completely true. It opens the door just a crack for a different experience to get in.

As you challenge the totality of your statement it will normally begin to weaken. Once it is weaker, this opens up opportunities. You can then start to discuss what needs to happen to capitalize on the small possibilities opened up. The emphatic belief expressed in the word 'never' will have changed to a belief that is less emphatic and more open to possibilities.

Another way to challenge such generalizations is to overstate them in order to demonstrate their absurdity. For example, in answer to 'I'll never be able to find the right partner,' you could say, 'Of course I'll never be able to find the right person. I mean, there are only about three billion members of the opposite sex and not one of them would suit me. Any that might suit me are obviously hiding, not wanting to get caught. All of those people joining dating agencies and going to singles parties are adamant they don't want to meet me, even though they don't know who I am.'

---

## Values

Values go together with beliefs. You value satisfying relationships, but what exactly does that mean to you? Here is an opportunity to explore.

What does a relationship need to have in order for it to work well for you? Do you need companionship, laughter, good sex, trust and freedom? What do you value in a relationship?

---

Make a list of all the things that are important to you in a relationship, all the qualities of the other person and all the qualities of the relationship. Ask yourself:

What do I value in a relationship?
What is important to me about a good relationship?
What do I get out of a good relationship?
What qualities should a good relationship have for me?
What matters to me in a relationship?
Do I want a relationship?

When you think about these questions, make sure you give answers that are true for you and not just answers that you would like to be true or are generally current or those that your friends have. Any values like this will only be your conditioned voice in another disguise, coming between you and what you really want. For values to mean anything they have to be yours – freely chosen and meaningful for you.

Now that you have these values, sort them into the more important ones and the less important ones.

Which five really stand out for you?
Are there some that are absolutely vital to you in order for a relationship to work?
Which ones do you really need in a relationship as opposed to the ones that you would like?

Look at these values carefully. They are probably quite abstract words such as 'love', 'trust', 'fun', 'sexual satisfaction', 'honesty', 'safety', 'laughter', 'security', 'excitement'. But what do these mean in practice? How do you know when you have them? What sort of actions are you looking for in a partner that let you know that these qualities are alive and well in your relationship?

For example, if you value honesty in a relationship, how do you know when you have it? How do you judge whether you have it?

You have to judge actions. What behaviour do you have to see or hear to know that you have an honest relationship? This may seem like a strange question, but values on their own are too abstract to judge. What matters is what you both do, not what you say. You also have to believe that your partner's actions really embody their values. You must be the judge of this.

---

There are two main ways in which people apply rules to values and judge others by them. One way of judging is to notice when the value is *absent*. So you take a certain level of honesty, for example, as given and then pay attention to when you see or hear something that lets you know that the relationship is no longer honest. The other way is not to take honesty for granted, but watch and listen for evidence that there is honesty. Also remember that these values are not absolute, either there or not. Nor may they be present all the time. You have to be the judge and you set the levels of what is acceptable to you. You may have to watch and listen a long time.

These are two very different approaches. It is much easier to start with assuming values and then noticing if they are absent. The danger of starting from the opposite direction is that you will always be looking or listening for evidence of love, affection or something else you value, and you may never be satisfied. Jealousy takes this approach to its extreme. Jealous people assume their partner is cheating on them, or is attracted to other people, and they need constant reassurance. The reassurance only lasts until their next suspicion.

If, after working out which values are the most important to you in relationships, you discover that the person you are with, or the sort of person you are looking for, has a number of the qualities of lower importance and none of those of higher importance, you may find yourself trying to change someone against their will or justifying staying with them because of something that is only slightly important to you. Your internal conditioned voice may say, 'All right, I know they're not honest with me and they sleep around, but they're great in company.' This will not work if honesty and fidelity are top values and sociability is of lower importance.

---

Take each of your important values in turn. We will use the example of being faithful to your partner. First apply the value to yourself, because it may be interesting to see whether you apply it in the same way as you do to your partner.

What actions of yours show that you are being faithful?
What actions of yours would show that you are not being faithful?
And which of the two do you pay more attention to?
Does being unfaithful mean kissing someone else?

    Having sex with them?

    Just wishing and fantasizing having sex with them?

    Do you have to initiate the contact for it to count as evidence?

Do you think in terms of being faithful or not being unfaithful?
Do thoughts count as well as actions?

Now switch your attention to your partner.

What do you look for in your partner that lets you know that they are faithful?
What do you look for in your partner that lets you know that they are not being faithful?
Which of the two do you pay more attention to?

And now, do you apply the same rules to your partner as you do to yourself?

---

If you have gone through these exercises, then it is likely to have taken some time, but you will be repaid with a much greater understanding of yourself and your partner. Read your answers through to yourself and notice any anomalies. Do you value honesty and believe the opposite sex is unable to be honest? Do you see yourself as gregarious and yet spend most evenings sitting watching television?

There are some foolproof recipes for unhappiness in relationships and they all come from not asking and therefore not knowing what your partner wants and values. The first way is to think that your partner values all the same things as you do, so you set about trying to satisfy them in the way that you wish that they would satisfy you. That way you will give them what you yourself want, not what they want. You need to know what is important to *your partner* and how to demonstrate it. Then you will be giving them what they want.

Secondly you need to tell your partner what is important to you and how they can demonstrate that, otherwise, how will they know? Unless you tell them, you will get from them what they imagine will satisfy you, based on their own values. They may be right, but they may not. Your relationship will be a lottery.

Here is a simple example. Suppose both you and your partner value demonstrating affection. The way you do this is to tell your partner you love them. And you want to hear that from them. This is the way you know that you are loved. Caresses, loving looks are not quite the same. Suppose your partner demonstrates their affection with caresses. Being told is not quite the same for them. Unless both of you are clear about what you value and tell the other, you will both feel dissatisfied. You will both be giving what you yourself want from the other and neither of you will be getting what you want. You both want to demonstrate affection, but each of you is giving what you want, and not getting what you want from the other. This is a simple example, but quite common.

Consider your rules about your values carefully. If you have a lot of rules about how your values can be violated and very few about how they can be met, then you will probably be dissatisfied with your relationships. This is not so much the relationship as the exact requirements you bring to it. It is extremely easy to be disappointed, simply by setting standards impossibly high. Perfectionism is one of the archenemies of relationships.

Some couples put themselves in a terrible double bind. One of them (let's say the woman, but it can be either) holds the value that the man must demonstrate love and that he should do so without ever being told that this is important and also without being told how to do it in a way that would satisfy her. Why? Because if the man loved her, then he should know automatically! Just imagine the convolutions and dissatisfaction those rules would generate. Since human beings are not natural mind readers, these people have set themselves up for failure by demanding some impossible mind reading.

Finally, make sure that your rules about values are easy to achieve. If the only way you can be sure that a man really loves you is if he climbs Mount Everest with your photograph in his breast pocket, then you are severely limiting your choice of partners.

These sorts of values confusion explain some 'inexplicable' divorces or separations, when one partner leaves in a flurry of negative emotion, saying they are unable to tolerate the situation anymore. How can this be? Usually neither person is getting what they really want from the relationship and they do not like what they *are* getting. In a real sense if you do not let your partner know what you want and how to give it to you, then you have no right to berate them, feel angry at them or feel they are at fault when they do not give it to you.

Take for an example where one partner's definition of happiness and their evidence that a relationship is working is:

We've stayed together.
We have financial security.
The children are well looked after.

We do not argue a lot.

Contrast this with the other partner's definition:

We have lots of fun.
We get filled with energy.
We have great sex.

In this example, suppose the first partner has their values met. They are happy. The other partner does not have their values met and they are not happy. When neither tells the other what they want but one simmers in discontent, then eventually one of three things happens. Either one partner will have had enough and will inexplicably (to the other partner, but maybe not to the world at large) leave. Secondly, both may resign themselves to lives filled with quiet desperation. Lastly, one or both may have an affair with someone who gives them the values that are missing from their lives. This is the reason for most affairs.

If there is one rule that comes up again and again as the most important for good relationships, it must be:

*Tell your partner what you want and what is important to you.*

Then:

*Give it to them if you can.*

If you find this very difficult, then there are many exercises in this book that will explore why this might be so.

This brings us to the crucial point of how you set your boundaries. For example, suppose you value honesty and faithfulness highly in a relationship. You are honest with your partner and faithful to them according to your own values. You tell them about your values and how important to you they are. However, you discover that your partner is having an affair and has lied to you about it. Now what do you do?

Your response will depend on your other values and also the boundaries you set. For some people, their partner indulging in even one affair would go beyond what they were willing to tolerate and they would separate from them. That one breach of trust would be serious enough on its own to go over the boundary of what they were willing to tolerate.

Other people might forgive. Although they might find that unfaithfulness deeply disturbing, the security of the relationship would be more important to them than just one affair and so they would choose to stay in the relationship. Perhaps the partner promises never to be unfaithful again. However, maybe a few months later, they *are* unfaithful again. Now what? They may be forgiven again. However, if it happens a third time, that pushes the relationship over the edge. Three strikes and they are out. In this case the person would have set their boundaries differently. What crosses the boundary is not the affair itself, but its repetition up to a crucial number, in this case three.

Take another couple in a similar position. The man is unfaithful once, twice, three times. Each time the woman is willing to forgive and to continue the relationship. However, one day she has had enough. It is not the number of times, but the fact that the infidelity has gone on over a long period, maybe months, maybe years. This woman has applied another sort of boundary – time. Not the number of times, but the length of time.

Sadly, in some cases the injured partner may find their boundaries have been crossed but have literally nowhere else to go and they feel trapped into staying whatever their other values.

---

Think about the sort of boundaries you have on your five important values.

Do you have a clear boundary for any of them – is there anything your partner could do, even if they did it *only once*, that would completely break the relationship for you? Is there anything you would not tolerate at all, whatever your partner said, however they excused themselves or however much they apologized?
If not, is there something you would tolerate for a certain number of times? How long would their behaviour have to continue before you had had enough?
What behaviour would breach your values if repeated over a long time period?
How many repetitions would it take before your boundary was breached, or how long would it have to go on for?

There is also the question of how badly your partner's behaviour violates your values as well as how long it goes on for. An example might be a woman who feels her partner is being unfaithful if he looks lustfully at another woman. She would leave immediately if he were to have a full affair, but his lustful glances also violate her values around fidelity, although to a lesser extent. She keeps telling him this, but he keeps doing it. Eventually she may leave him because she cannot stand it any longer.

So, there are three types of boundary:

how important the situation is to you: intensity
how many times it happens: repetition
how long it goes on for: duration

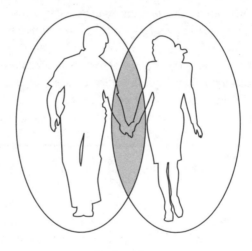

Our boundaries

It is important you set your boundaries and know what they are to avoid several dangers in relationships. The first danger is setting your boundaries too close – in other words, having many different trivial forms of behaviour that violate your boundaries immediately. For example, a man may not tolerate his girlfriend flirting with another man even once. He may not tolerate her even talking to another man at a party. He may not even be able to tolerate other men giving her admiring glances, thinking that in some way she is leading them on. He may not leave her, but he may punish her by being unkind, or even violent.

So boundaries that are too low can cause a lot of trouble between couples. They may be too low if all sorts of trivial actions breach the boundaries, or the person can only tolerate them happening a few times, or over a very short period.

The second danger is having boundaries that are too distant, maybe so distant that to all intents and purposes there are no boundaries at all. This results in too much trust and leaves a person open to being exploited and abused. Such a person is too willing to forgive and forget time after time. The other person takes far more from the relationship than they put in and may start to think they can get away with anything. They behave more and more outrageously, like a naughty child pushing the limits, seeing where the boundaries are. The worst case would be where one partner was willing to keep forgiving the other because they lacked well-defined boundaries. They would tolerate the situation in order to keep the relationship. In the end, the other partner might well leave them, accusing them of being too tolerant or too weak.

We all need boundaries. We need to have them for ourselves and we need to have them for others. Sometimes the cost of hanging on to a relationship is just too high. There are times when giving up is the right thing to do.

---

## REALITY CHECK

Now for a reality check on how effective you are at putting your insights into operation. To do this, think back and make a list of the partners you have had throughout your life. If you have only had a few or none, list the people you have found attractive.

Take a piece of paper and divide it in two from top to bottom. On one side put the heading 'positive qualities' and on the other 'negative qualities'. Take the first name on your list of partners and write down both their positive and negative qualities under the relevant headings. Then take the second named partner and repeat the process, ticking a quality which has already appeared in the list in connection with an earlier partner. Continue this process until you have analysed everyone on your list.

This list will give you a reality check on what you actually select for, as opposed to what you believe you select for.

For instance, when you defined your criteria you may have decided that honesty was the most important quality that you look for in a partner. Having analysed previous partners you may find that relatively few of them possessed honesty.

If there is a difference, this will show the separation between what you believe to be your criteria and how in reality your conditioned voice guides you.

Also look for any disadvantages of what you select for and if any of the qualities might clash with each other. For example, if you are looking for an adventurous type who is also home-loving, you may find it hard to get both qualities in one person.

## Identity

Finally to the identity level – you as a whole person.

Write down a brief description of how you see yourself in the context of relationships, for example, 'I am an affectionate lover' or 'I am a trustworthy person' or 'I am someone who gives more than they receive' or, on the other hand, 'I'm hard hearted' or 'I'm the sort of person who gets taken for granted' or 'I love them and leave them.'

Whatever your way of describing yourself, play with the descriptions until your find one that really fits. It might be enlightening or a restatement of something you have known for ages.

Write down the statement you finish with:

'I am … in relationships.'

Now think what sort of metaphor would describe you.

What is your identity like? Is it like a whirlwind? An affectionate pet? A Don Juan?

'In relationships I am like … because…'

What else has to be true for this metaphor to make sense?

Now think of a metaphor of what you would like to be:
   'In relationships, I would like to be ... because...'

How does your first metaphor relate to the second?
Also, how well is your identity supported by what you have discovered in the other levels?

Having written down your sense of self, think for a while about how that awareness has affected your relationships in the past. It may be one of the causes of your success. It might be one factor that has limited you or established the repetition of unwanted patterns within your relationships. For example, someone I knew had an identity of 'I'm a loner.' He lived out that identity – even in the midst of others.

# 3

# Our Intellectual Voice

■ The intellectual voice is our capacity to evaluate, to take a step outside the feelings of the present, to compare and decide. It is not swayed either by instinct or blind conditioning. It is not about academic knowledge, higher mathematics, formal education or philosophy. It is reasonable, although not necessarily logical. It does not stand in contrast to emotions, but works with them. It is certainly not somehow superior to our emotions and will not necessarily make the right decision left to itself. Often we will act purely on our emotions, against the counsel of reason, and we will be right to do so. You need a balance between emotion and reason for your relationships to be most fulfilling. A strong intellectual voice is an essential part of that balance.

The intellectual voice needs something to work on – like fire, it can't burn without fuel and it burns poorly on low-grade fuel. Serve it up conflicting and limiting beliefs, confused values and mistaken facts and it will do its best, but its conclusion will be as good as the fuel. The intellectual voice needs accurate information to work from. Give it a false belief and it will spin hundreds of justifications and courses of action from that belief.

Our intellectual voice is the basis of our science and technology and it also has a place in affairs of the heart. You know for yourself that rational thought is the first casualty of our more basic urges.

The three voices develop in sequence as we mature. When we are born, our behaviour is largely instinctual. As we grow, so we absorb cultural and family beliefs, values and behaviour, and the conditioned voice slots into place. And as this happens the capacity for intellectual thought develops. We know from psychological studies that abstract reasoning is fairly late to develop, that young children do not think rationally. Each layer builds on the last. We cannot learn to be social without our basic needs being met. And we cannot think straight without a solid foundation in language and learning from our culture, society and family. We set great store by our intellect. However, it is the last faculty to develop in our journey to adulthood and it comes from a part of the brain that is an evolutionary afterthought, the latest arrival in its millions of years of evolution. We doubt whether mankind has had enough practice yet to be very good at pure reasoning.

Intellect allows us to think *about* things and not be lost *in* them. We can hold one thought while comparing it with another and evaluate feelings, even those strong feelings that come from the deeper part of the brain about hunger, thirst, sex and even survival. A child will not give its life for an idea, but a man or woman may.

The intellect tends to be more highly prized by men than women, and traditionally men have achieved more in the intellectual fields of academic subjects. We doubt the reason is that women are less good at them, if they put their minds to it, although there are gender differences between the brains of men and women that do account for some of the differences in their achievements. This is a minefield of speculation as well as prejudice. Men and women are better at different things and this is only a problem if you think they are in competition.

How familiar are you with your intellectual voice? You probably know it quite well; it is a good friend. The intellectual voice is the rational, evaluating and calm voice that gathers information and makes unbiased decisions and recommendations. It tells us what is right, based on the information available to it, not what we would like to be right.

---

Imagine for a moment that you have to make a choice. Make it a simple choice with no emotional content, for example, will you finish this section of the book now or later?

How did you go about making that choice?
What does this voice of the intellect sound like?
Does it seem to come from outside you or inside?
Which side of you does it seem to come from, or is it central?
Does it seem to come from above you or below you?

What sort of voice is it?
Was there one clear internal voice or were there two or more voices
arguing the merits?
If you hear two voices, where do they come from?
Are the choices represented as pictures?
Is there a feeling associated with the choice – did you 'weigh' up the
alternatives?

Whatever you did would involve evaluating the possibilities without having to commit to any of them. There is no great passion attached to reading the rest of the section or not, which makes it that much easier to pass
from one choice to another. If one choice had a lot of emotion attached,
it would be harder. You would have to disengage yourself from it to look
at the other choices.

---

The intellectual voice involves two skills:

1  Disengaging from an idea, putting aside the feeling and moving on
   to another choice.
2  Making a choice based on an overall evaluation once you have
   looked them all over.

For some people it is like being above all the possibilities and looking
down on them. For others, it is like weighing the points of view; there
is an element of feeling in how they decide. For others, it is like hearing all the viewpoints – perhaps they talk to themselves, representing
different viewpoints with different voices or with the same voice coming from different places in their mind. You can sometimes see people
doing this in a kind of internal argument, first cocking their head
to one side, looking puzzled, then turning their head the other way to
hear a different viewpoint, like a judge in a court of law listening
to two barristers.

The intellectual voice is vital to the success of relationships. You need
it to restrain the instinctive voice when it shows you a road to instant
gratification, to check that there is not future pain around the next bend.
You need it to evaluate what your conditioned voice is suggesting, to
compare what works and what does not, what is empowering and what is

not. Intellect can take a position outside these issues, so we are not blindly caught in them.

Mister Spock from *Star Trek* must represent the archetypal intellectual voice. In *Star Trek*, Captain Kirk had to somehow harmonize intellect, symbolized by Mister Spock, and emotion, symbolized by Doctor McCoy. This is a good metaphor, because emotion without guidance is like a runaway horse, all power but no direction. Intellect without emotion is like a big psychology textbook, lots of ideas, but no soul, and also big and thick enough to beat someone over the head with to subdue them. Relationships based only on what is sensible are likely to be dry, uninspiring, without love and passion. We may enter into sensible relationships because our parents have always taught us to be sensible; this would be a case of the intellect and conditioning working together. If genetic drives or conditioning are ignored in favour of being sensible, though, we may end up in an emotional refrigerator.

## NEW PERSPECTIVES

The intellectual voice does have two enormous strengths. First, it can stand apart from feelings and evaluate them by comparison. It can hold two ideas without being drawn into either of them. It can think *about* ideas and not be lost *in* them; it can hold them at arm's length and decide what to do.

Secondly, it is a time traveller. It can stand aside from the present, jump into the possible (and probable) future and look back and judge from that perspective whether what you want to do is a good idea. It can imagine different futures. It can travel into the past and use that experience to help.

Boy meets girl at a party, for instance. He flirts with her and she flirts back. However she already has a large muscular boyfriend. The boy remembers the last time this happened the boyfriend took him outside and beat him up. 'Go on,' whispers the genetic voice, 'it'll be OK.' But the boy imagines what might happen to him if this boyfriend got angry and decides to flirt with someone else, despite his sexual excitement.

A woman might be very attracted to a married man, perhaps even start an affair with him, and then realize that the relationship, built as it is on secrecy and mistrust, has no long-term future. She may also realize that if the man is cheating on his wife, he may also cheat on her.

The balance between our intellect and our emotions is difficult, because they are not using the same sort of values to judge by. Emotion decides by strength of bodily feeling in the present. Intellect considers longer-term scenarios.

The intellectual voice can stand outside time and trace out possible consequences. Both the conditioned voice and the genetic voice come from the past and blind us in the present. If we have a problem in the present, we can think back to the past to find the causes, perhaps pinpoint the bad decision we made or see a pattern of increasing dissatisfaction. Perhaps it was not just one instance but a slow pattern building up, imperceptible at the time, but obvious with hindsight. If only we could have foreseen it! Our intellect lets us do this – we do not foresee the future exactly, but we can spin out some likely consequences.

Imagine time as a long line. We talk about long and short times, going far into the past and future, the length of time. Whatever time really is, we tend to think of it in terms of length. The intellectual voice is our time-travelling guide, like Doctor Who, showing us a possible future and helping us understand the past, a traveller up and down the timeline.

With the intellect we can take different perspectives, we can imagine what something is like from another person's point of view, and this gives us the basis of empathy.

We have our own perspective – this is called 'first position' in NLP. First position is important, part of our identity, but if it were the whole story we would all be egoistic monsters. We take a first position before we take others' feelings into account and so it is allied to the genetic voice. It is about our needs, our viewpoint and our beliefs.

We can also take a 'second position' and identify with others. This we acquire from our society, family and culture; it is the basis of fellow feeling. Anyone without these shared feelings will not care for or about other people, because other people only exist as means to fulfil their own desires and needs. These people are usually labelled psychopaths or sociopaths. So second position develops from the shared experience in society and is allied with the conditioned voice.

The 'third position' comes from the intellectual voice. It is not taking someone else's point of view, but the ability to take another point of view entirely and judge between different viewpoints.

## RIGHTS AND RESPONSIBILITIES

The intellectual voice usually has a lot to say about rights and responsi-bilities. We are all keen to establish our rights, but not so keen to take on responsibilities. Yet we all have responsibilities as well as rights and sometimes couples quarrel over them.

There are some typical gender differences here too. Men tend to emphasize rights. They tend to value independence more than women and rights are something that define you as independent, you have them just by being you. We know men who assume that because they are out work-ing all day, they have the right to stay late with their mates in the bar after work, but these sort of rights are often not agreed by both partners.

Women are more drawn towards responsibilities because responsi-bilities are how you respond to someone else and women tend to favour relationships above the masculine values of strength, power and inde-pendence. So while rights are more about independence, responsibilities are more relational. Yet neither can exist without the other. Having rights means you also have responsibilities and vice versa. Men often fall into the trap of assuming their rights and forgetting the responsibil-ities that go with them.

A relationship gives both parties equal rights and responsibilities and it is worth being clear about them. You may be clear in your own mind, but rights are granted and responsibilities are given, so both sides need to be clear. If you think you have a right and your partner does not, then there will be trouble, just as if you think your partner has a responsibility but they do not think so.

---

Experiment with this exercise:

What rights do you think you have in your relationship? Make a list.
Now imagine you are your partner in the relationship. Go to their perspective (second position).
From your partner's perspective, do you agree with this list?
Still from your partner's viewpoint, what responsibilities would you expect to go with these rights?
Now, from your point of view again, what responsibilities do you think you have to your partner?

What do you take care of?
What household jobs do you do?
Who earns the money?
Who looks after the money?
What other responsibilities do you perceive you have?
Make a list of your responsibilities, as you perceive them.
Now, from your partner's perspective, what responsibilities do they expect from you?
Now make a comparison of your lists (third position). They can make very interesting reading. Check them out with your partner for real if they show a large discrepancy.

---

Again, balance is important. The trap for men is to assume rights and not to think of responsibilities. For women, it tends to be the opposite, to assume responsibilities and neglect their corresponding rights.

## MORE THAN WORDS

Good communication starts with the intellectual voice, but it brings in the other voices too. We may set out to communicate something intellectually and finish in a flaming argument, wondering how such a simple idea could lead to such a quarrel. One way this can happen is through escalation up the logical levels. Be very careful with this – every time you move up a level, you up the ante significantly, for each level brings more emotion with it.

For example, let's say a woman is sitting in the living-room and her husband comes in. He says, 'This room is really untidy.'

This could be a simple observation, on the level of the environment, but life is not that simple. The wife sees it as an implicit criticism of her.

'I tidied it this morning,' she replies.

Two things have happened. The first is that she has accepted responsibility for the state of the room and secondly, she has moved up to the level of behaviour to defend herself.

Her husband could escalate and say, 'Well, you certainly didn't do it very well!'

(He might also have assumed the right to sit down in a tidy room after work.)

Now he is questioning her ability to keep the house tidy and this may be an important value of hers.

She might say, 'If you helped more, instead of criticizing, then it would be easier!'

(She does not accept his right either.)

And then we would have reached the identity level if he were to respond, 'Are you saying I'm critical? I haven't mentioned it in weeks [implying he has noticed and thought about it]. Don't be so sensitive!'

So, having started with the environment, we are now in an identity battle – being critical against being sensitive.

Communication is sharing something and involves much more than just an exchange of facts. So the intellectual voice on its own is not enough – it will confuse information with communication. Information is telling something, but communication involves meaning and influence. We cannot not communicate; even silence is a communication. We know at least one couple where silence is a very bad sign. When the wife is silent, her husband and children tiptoe around like bomb disposal experts waiting for the inevitable explosion.

Communication is how you build your relationship or destroy it. Misunderstandings happen because what goes on inside our heads is invisible to others, so good communication means doing two things:

1 Sharing your expectations, beliefs and values, explaining your experience so your partner can understand it. We all expect others to navigate our world, but often keep the map locked behind our eyebrows.

2 Asking questions so you can understand your partner's expectation and values, so you can get a glimpse of their map and not have to travel blindly through their world.

We communicate with more than just words. Our tone of voice and body language tell our partner what the words mean. That is why when asked if we love someone it is possible to *say*, 'Of course I love you,' and *convey* 'I'm really annoyed you're asking me that again' or 'You're all right' or 'I'd die if you left me' and many more meanings through changes in our inflection or body language. Words are just the start of communication.

When the words and the non-verbal signals convey different messages, it is the non-verbal message that we believe. We may pretend to respond to the words and sometimes we pretend not to notice the body language because it is embarrassing and difficult to deal with the clash between it and the words. But deep down we know something is not right.

I (Robin) remember watching cowboy films when I was young. They were the simple sort when the good guy wore a white hat and was polite to ladies. The bad guys wore black hats, were unshaven and looked sideways at everyone. Their shoulders slouched when they saw the good guys. Three quarters of the way through the film, there would be a gunfight between the white hats and the black hats where each would hide behind a wall with no way of getting a clear shot at the other. Then they would talk to each other. The bad guy would always make a promise to surrender to encourage the good guy to break his cover. 'OK, Clint, you've got me cornered. I'm coming out, don't shoot.' The good guy would then pretend to show himself. The bad guy would then jump out and take a shot, and then the good guy, using all the guile invested in him by goodness, would nip back behind the wall and let the bad guy have it.

Many couples trying to resolve issues adopt the same strategy. Consequently only one of them can win. Winning means someone loses and that can harm the relationship. If you genuinely want to communicate, it requires trust and the desire for life to be better for both of you. If communication becomes a game of words, a verbal tennis match, where one of you is victorious and the other is left confused and manipulated, then you both lose.

### Questions

Questions are an important way of communicating. There are many ways to ask questions. If you watch political reporters and interviewers it will give you an appreciation of how difficult questioning can be and how distorted the answers can be when the questioning is of a poor quality.

I (Joseph) remember some years ago being interviewed for television. The interviewer asked me the questions and I answered. All the time the camera was rolling. The interview went well. I was pleased.

When it was over, the cameraman then filmed the interviewer asking the questions again. These bits of film were spliced in to replace the questions I responded to. I was surprised, but it makes sense because when you see a television interviewer ask a question, the camera is usually on them while they do so. Then it switches to the person being interviewed. This technique would be fine if the questions that the interviewer asked to camera the second time were the same as she asked me the first time. They were not quite the same and what came over in the edited film footage was that I was being evasive because I did not answer the question the interviewer put to me.

There is a parallel to this in relationships. When we ask a question, sometimes the question that our partner answers is not the same question as we understand it. In relationships, the quality of questioning will influence how close you become to your partner and the amount of trust that can grow between you.

We ask questions for one of two main reasons. The first reason is to establish the truth and understand what is going on with the other person. The second reason is to get the other person to say what we want them to say, what it would suit us for them to say. The first style is honest. The second is dishonest and manipulative. However the biggest mistake that most manipulative questioners make is not the manipulation itself, it is that they act upon the manipulated answer as if it were the truth. The reasoning goes: 'Now that I have engineered someone to tell me they love me I can act as if they love me' or 'Now that I've forced someone to tell me they'll always be faithful I can assume and act as though they will always be faithful.' A forced reply to a manipulative question is not worth the air that carries it from mouth to ear.

What separates manipulation from persuasion or guidance? Your intention. If you are asking questions to guide someone to consider other possibilities with the intention of helping them, then that is guidance. If the only party who gains is you, then that is manipulation.

When it comes to gathering information there are seven very useful words: 'what', 'where', 'how', 'when', 'which', 'who' and 'why'. A 'yes' or a 'no' cannot answer any question that begins with one of these words. They demand fuller answers. If you provide the space for someone to answer and do not rush in with a supplementary questions then these seven words will gain a great deal of information. However, you'd best be careful of the word 'why'. Why be careful? To find out, answer the following questions in your head:

When was the last time you went on holiday?
Where did you go?
What was the weather like?
Which travel company did you book through?
How long did you go for?
Whom did you go with?
Why did you go with that person or people, or why did you go alone?

The first six questions seek out factual information. The question 'why' seeks out the rationale behind a decision. Although this is useful information to have, getting it can be seen as confrontational. You force people to justify actions and decisions. This form of question can also be received as criticism. This is especially so during a heated conversation.

By all means be critical and accusatory if it suits you both. But you may like to consider using one of the other words to take the place of the 'why' and ask questions such as: 'What's behind doing it that way?' or 'How were you expecting that to work?' or 'What's important about that?' The difference may seem small but the effect is important.

## THE LANGUAGE OF THE SENSES

We ask questions and listen to the answers, and we also get information through our five senses. Without them we would have no evidence that anything existed.

People make use of these senses in varying amounts. The most commonly dominant senses are sight, hearing and touch. The two that are usually of lesser importance as information gathering channels are taste and smell. This is not always the case. For instance a chef, wine taster or tea grader is likely to have a greater sensitivity to tastes and smells than the rest of us. A musician is likely to have a higher than normal predisposition to sound. A film director or artist might be more visually dominant and might also have the ability to detach themselves from what is taking place, automatically adopting that objective position.

If we have a dominant sense it will be very important to us and we will express that importance in the language that we use. If you asked someone who is very visual about a holiday they are likely to tell you about the setting of their accommodation, the colours of the scenery, the amount of cloud in the sky and what their bedroom looked like. Somebody who is more sound orientated is likely to tell you about the birdsong, whether the local nightclubs were noisy and about the folk music of the area. A feeling person will emphasize the amount of traffic in the streets, how hot the weather was or how crowded the beach. Most people will give you a mixture or balance of these sensory descriptions.

What has this to do with relationships? Do you know what sensory preferences your partner has? If you do not, you may be limiting the effectiveness of your communication with them. Here is a short conversation between the husband and wife we met earlier, again about the untidy house.

'This house *looks* untidy.'
'But it *feels* comfortable like this.'
'But *imagine* if a friend called and *saw* it like this.'
'They'd know it was a *relaxed* home.'
'How could people turn a *blind eye* to rubbish like this?'
'They could if they were *at ease* with each other.'

They are both talking about the same thing, the condition of their home, but putting different interpretations on what it means. One sees mess that means sloppiness, the other feels comfort and love. Because neither is using the other's sensory language they do not agree. They are unable to understand each other.

Very often one person hates untidiness while the other literally does not see it. As long as they are comfortable, or they are too busy talking to themselves or engaged in conversation to care about the state of the room, they do not worry. In this sort of situation, to get through to them you have to speak their sensory language. So you would have to say something like, 'I know that you don't put much store on how the room looks, but for me it's like sitting down on a hard chair. I just can't get comfortable.' Anyone who is into feeling more strongly will grasp this immediately. It will become real for them in a way it was not before. With someone for whom hearing is more important, you might say, 'I know you don't listen to me when I say the room is untidy, but for me it's just like listening to a faulty CD, the music keeps going out of tune and rhythm. It grates on my nerves.'

Although tidiness may seem like a small part of what makes a relationship work, it is the small things that annoy, because they often share the same roots as larger misunderstandings and happen more often. If you feel you will not be understood on small points you may give up seeking mutual understanding on the big points.

Listen to your partner talking to other people at a time when you do not need to be paying attention to what exactly they say. Notice if you can identify words that they use that can be associated with any of the five senses. Over a period of time you may identify a preference. If you do, use those words when talking to them and see if there is any change or improvement in your ability to understand and be understood. It might be that saying 'Can you see my point?' would make more sense to your partner than 'I want you to know how I feel.'

Sensory preference also plays a part in sexual activity and expressing affection. Not surprisingly, people with a dominant sense of sight prefer visual stimulation as part of foreplay. Others prefer words or touching. If your partner is visual, then how you dress and look will be important. If they place more emphasis on words, then what you say and how you say it will influence how stimulated they become. And if touching is important – well, touching is always important, but it is more important to some than others.

# 4

# Intelligent Harmony

■ Now we have our three voices. What sort of harmony do they create? They rarely have a completely solo spot, although one may dominate, depending on the circumstances. You might also think of them as
colours in a palette – the deep red of the instinctive voice, the blue of
the conditioned voice and the pale green of the intellectual voice.
What sort of picture can you paint?

Everyone has their own harmony. Everyone paints their own picture,
because these are not fixed faculties, but fluid types of intelligence.
When they blend together well they make you intelligent – sexually,
emotionally, socially and intellectually.

Each of the voices alone has its characteristic weaknesses. The
genetic voice cares only for the moment and gratification. The conditioned voice may bring all the weaknesses and short-sightedness and
insularity of your society, culture and parents, and all the limiting
beliefs about yourself and false conclusions that those bring. The intellect on its own is dry, unexciting and can only give answers based on
the quality of the information it works with. Left to itself it is like the
endless paperwork of the mind.

Each of the voices has its strengths, too. The genetic voice has
energy, drive and urgency. The conditioned voice has social skills, communication skills and empowering beliefs and values. The intellectual
voice has judgement, objectivity, time travel and evaluation abilities.
Put them together with your emotions and feelings and you have intelligent harmony.

With the model of the three voices, how might a relationship work?
You see someone and your genetic voice responds. It whispers about
the colour of their eyes, the shape of their body, the music of their

voice and the way they move. You feel a tumbling in your stomach, an excitement, maybe a slight perspiring, and you can't take your eyes off them. You turn away but your eyes find their way back. You judge, unknowingly, that according to the criteria accepted as being attractive you and this other person are similar. Not only do they stir you, but they also seem familiar, as if they would have fitted into your childhood home. They look like the person you have mentally rehearsed for all your life. You play eye games to establish mutual attraction. They are the sort you always go for. You make your way, as if by accident, to be near each other. You start talking. Over time, you find you have a lot in common. Your view of the world, what is important and what is true for you are similar. What that other person is looking for in life is compatible with what you want. They have the same definition of relationship as you. They like to do the things that you like and go to the places you enjoy. You go out together. It feels good. It seems you both can help each other be more of who you want to be. You feel more complete. In the cold light of day your objective assessment is that it could work between you. Your three voices are all satisfied and can sing together and be compatible with this other person's three voices. This coming together happens all the time. Sometimes, however, life is not this simple.

There is no future in a relationship without some degree of trust. The most satisfying relationships mean sharing, learning about the other person, telling them about yourself. You let another person into your life, first by opening the door a little and then, if trust develops, opening it more fully and letting them in. In the same way, you slowly get to know them. You never tell everyone everything about yourself, but trust means being honest about what you choose to tell and being open about what concerns you both and what is important to you both in a relationship. You do not need trust to have sex, the genetic voice alone does not need it, but you do need trust if sex is to become more than just physical pleasure, and if the other person is to be more than a physical body to give you enjoyment.

The word 'trust' comes from an Old Norse word meaning 'strong'. In other words, we develop trust when we believe we can rely on the strength of the other person to hold us; they will not drop us or let us down. 'Trust' and 'true' come from the same root word. What we trust becomes true for us and what is true we trust. Very rarely do we trust someone immediately; trust takes time to develop. Developing trust is like bringing up children – as they demonstrate more and more by example that they can be trusted, so we give them a looser and looser rein. We test the other person to know that they will not let us down, not by necessarily setting them a special trial, but by seeing how they deal with life.

There is always a risk to trust. That is what makes it so precious. How do you build a relationship of trust? How do you know that the other person is being honest with you, that they mean what they say? How can you know that they are telling you the truth, telling you what they really feel rather than what you want to hear, or, worse, spinning you a tissue of lies to hide what they really think? To commit to a relationship, even in the short term, we need to feel safe and trust is what makes us safe.

The reality of life is that people are not necessarily trustworthy. Indiscriminate and immediate trust is foolish. However, while there are no easy answers, there are some useful ground rules about trust we can use as our guides.

First, trust must have boundaries. Trust without a boundary is not really trust at all, but an indiscriminate openness. Trust has to be won and granted fairly to be worthwhile. We have already dealt with setting your boundaries over what you will tolerate, how many times and over how long *(see p.72)*. Sometimes you have to take a decision to put up with what you have or to leave the relationship. You have to ask yourself the question: 'Am I prepared to stay in this relationship if nothing changes?' This is the worst case. If you are, then stay. If not, then you need to leave.

Also, trust is not an all or nothing state. You can grant it in some areas but not others. There are some people you might trust with your money but not with your partner. Some people you would trust with your partner, but not to mend a fuse.

Secondly, separate trust from rapport, affection and especially sexual attraction. I (Joseph) remember in particular two friends I used to know. They were charming companions, I liked them a lot and enjoyed their company, but they were unreliable in many ways and I never trusted them. Do not confuse trust with wanting to trust. We may want to trust someone because they are so attractive, charming and good to be with, but these are their qualities. Take them and enjoy them, but do not trust someone just because you would like to.

Thirdly, trust develops over time, not from what people say but from what they do. Trust cannot be bought – you give it freely or it is earned. When you trust someone, it means in part that they are constant, they are reliable, they are recognizably the same from day to day. When they make a promise one day, they are the same person the next day to honour it.

Here is a paradox. In order to be trustworthy a person has to be flexible, has to learn and has to have the ability to change. Why? Because life is not the same from day to day, conditions change and we have to learn to change with them in order to be reliable. Without this ability to change a person is too rigid, inflexible, unable to adapt to circumstances. It is like a tree bending in the wind. The way trees stay alive and upright against all the weather conditions is not by being rigid and inflexible, but by being able to go with the weather conditions. To be trustworthy, we have to be capable of self-renewal. Beware of trusting people who are extremely rigid, who have to have things done always the same way, who expect you to adapt to them all the time, rather than giving and taking.

Fourthly, trust cannot flourish when you are afraid. If you ever feel afraid of the other person, of what they might do to you, then it is very hard to trust and usually they have not earned your trust.

Lastly, regard your trust as precious, not to be given lightly. Trust is like glass – once it is broken it cannot be replaced exactly as it was. Trust is earned. Never allow someone to make you feel guilty for not trusting them. That is a danger sign. Anyone who becomes upset or is oversensitive about being trusted may have something to hide.

What if you trust someone and they let you down badly and the relationship breaks down? This is intensely painful. Not only do you lose the other person, and the relationship you wanted, but also it can threaten your self-esteem. We rely on others to build our self-esteem – the more others love and cherish us, the better we feel and the stronger our self-esteem. There are very few people whose self-esteem is so solidly build on the own opinion of themselves that it is immune to what other people think. Healthy self-esteem is a balance between knowing and loving ourselves and paying attention to what other people think. Other people are like mirrors – we hold ourselves up to them to get another perspective on what we are like. However, some people are distorting mirrors – they do not reflect our true worth.

If someone deceives you badly, then it seems they must have valued you very little. Does that mean you are of little value? No. Just because someone else doesn't value you, it does not mean that you are worthless. It mean only that, for whatever reason, that person did not value you and that can say a lot about them and not very much about you at all. Breaking a relationship does not mean that your identity is rejected. It may mean that the other person cannot get on with you on the other levels – beliefs and values, capabilities, behaviour or even environment. Or they may be untrustworthy and deceive you for their own reasons – reasons that you might never know. However badly they acted, presumably they had a reason good enough to convince themselves. Somehow they made a choice that made sense to them in some strange way. People make the best choice they can based on the world as they see it. However, some people see the world awry, like distorting mirrors, and it appears very different to them than it does to you or most other people.

You may have been deceived and you did not see it coming. You may start to question your judgement and lose confidence. How could you have been so stupid? How can you ever be sure of anyone again? You need time to recover. When the initial pain has abated, you can engage your intellectual voice to help you understand what has happened. You need to ask yourself some hard questions:

Why me?
>    Was there anything that I did that made it easy for them to deceive
>    me?
Why now?
>    What happened in my life recently, or what changed recently, so
>    that I was deceived then rather than at any other time?
Why did they lie?
>    What sort of world do they see themselves living in that justified
>    what they did, at least in their own eyes? You will not agree with
>    them, but you may begin to understand how they thought.
Were there any reasons why I wanted to believe them rather than be
more cautious?

These questions will help you to learn from the experience so that it will not happen again.

How can you develop a sense of when to trust? We all have some intuition about who is trustworthy – a sixth sense. Women have developed, on the whole, a better sense of intuition because, being physically weaker, they needed to be more in tune with the moods and attitudes of men. So they became better at reading and understanding the messages conveyed by body language and voice qualities. Even in the days of grunting, different grunts meant different things. Women reached a higher level of expertise in taking information from their five senses, wrapping them all together in an instant and making meaning out of them. However, we all have this 'knowing'. It is often called 'gut reaction'. It is the ability to pick out changes in pattern, alterations to the norm, and interpret the meaning of those changes. We apply this ability to our relationships – though sometimes we choose to ignore such signals because we don't know what to do with them.

Your intuition not only keeps you out of difficult relationships, but also gives you the confidence to commit in a relationship. Your intuition will protect you. How do you develop it?

First give yourself some mental space. This means not trusting everyone indiscriminately. Do not assume everyone is trustworthy. Let your trust be earned. On the other hand, do not automatically assume that people are not to be trusted. Everybody is different. If one partner lets you down that does not mean that the next will as well. All the partners might have in common is finding you attractive.

Without strong expectations and preconceived ideas you will be more open to seeing, hearing and feeling the person in the moment. Really pay attention to them. What body language do they have? Does it match with their words? We do not think that there are universal signals in body language that tell you when someone is lying. In other words, when a person crosses their arms in front of them, it need not mean they are being defensive. They may have another gesture when they are being defensive. When someone scratches their nose it does not automatically mean that they are lying. They may just have an itch. Body language does not have a fixed meaning. That would be too simplistic. However, each person's body language is consistent. To interpret it, you have to get to know them and look and listen to them in many circumstances to see the patterns. So, for example, if you notice that your partner has a habit of shifting their weight onto the

right side of their body when they lie, be suspicious if they do that
when they are talking to you!

How do we read and interpret other people's body language and
voice quality? You are already doing it. If you have a partner you will
know when their mood changes and what that change means. Without
looking out for change, you will notice variations in behaviour, maybe
something in the weight of their footstep, how they pick up a paper, an
intake of breath or a thousand and one details that all tell you that there
is something happening.

Turn the sound down on the television and notice how much you
can tell about people and the state they are in by their facial expression.
When you are talking to someone on the phone, notice how far you
interpret the conversation not by the words that are said but by the way
they are said.

The eyes convey many messages. The loss of direct eye contact is
often seen as being shifty or dishonest. This may be so, but not necessarily. As with all non-verbal signals, eye movement is individual.
However, if someone's eyes dip down to their left, this most commonly
means that they have broken eye contact in order to have an internal
dialogue with themselves. If to their right, they are checking out their
feelings about what you are discussing. Indeed, the superior oblique
muscle that turns the eyeball downwards is called the pathetic muscle.
We say someone looks pathetic when in fact they are checking inwardly how they feel about something. If you are talking to someone and
their eyes do turn downwards, then give them time to mull over whatever they are dealing with. When it is time to talk again their eyes will
rise to meet yours. You can find out more about how body language
shows how we think from the NLP books listed at the back of this
book.

Pay attention to your intuition. You may not understand it, but do
not dismiss it. A number of times we have heard friends describe how
they were deceived and then say something like, 'Well, it seemed a bit
odd at the time and I felt a bit strange about it, but I didn't really pay
any attention to it.'

Notice how your partner acts with their family and friends and if
other people trust them. If a person has let others down in the past, they
may let you down as well.

There are also some warning signals that may make you think twice about trusting someone. Again, these are generalizations. They are not necessarily significant, but we have found them to be useful pointers.

Think twice before trusting if the other person is very rigid. It may mean that they are not able to adapt easily and may only be trustworthy if their circumstances do not change.

Does the other person make you feel afraid? Do they make you feel guilty about not trusting them? Neither of these is a secure basis for trust.

Romantic relationships can lead to betrayal and bitterness, but also to fun, affection, love. We believe fundamentally that they are worth the effort.

How can you be trustworthy? What is the secret of projecting the right non-verbal message? Be honest. Know your boundaries. Decide what you want to share and share it. Tell your partner how you feel. You need not tell your partner everything you feel, but whatever you do decide, be honest. Your partner may well have an intuition when you are not. When you are honest, your body language will match your words.

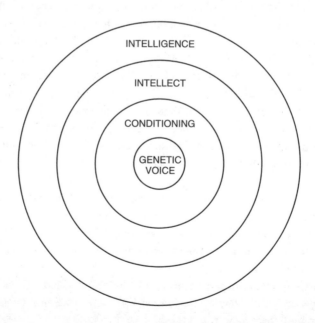

Balancing the voices

## BALANCING THE VOICES IN A RELATIONSHIP JOURNEY

When the voices are in intelligent harmony, you will also be 'congruent', the different parts of yourself working together, making a beautiful tapestry in which all the colours fit and do not clash. Congruence, like trust, is not an all or nothing state of affairs; you can be more or less congruent. This exercise will explore how you know when you are congruent about committing to a relationship with someone and how much congruence you feel. How much congruence you feel will tell you how much you trust the other person.

---

First, think of a situation (within a relationship if you like, but that is not essential), when you were absolutely sure that what you were doing was the right thing for you. You may have been excelling at some activity or just having fun or being totally immersed in where you wanted to be.

Re-create the scene for yourself, closing your eyes if necessary, and make the picture as realistic as you can. Be back in that scene. See it again through your own eyes.

Now make sure you are apart from it, seeing yourself in the situation, or viewing it from a different perspective from the one you had at the time.

Now re-create all the sounds associated with the scene. Hear the background noise, other voices, what your internal voice is saying, any music that may be playing and any other sounds that are relevant.

Re-create any tastes and smells.

Now, what are your feelings as you do this?

Do this with two other situations where you felt completely congruent about what you were doing or the decision you made.

Now you can view all three instances.

What was present in all three?

What has to be there, in you, for you to be congruent?

It could be a particular sort of feeling, hard to classify. It might be a particular quality of picture or sound. It might be a certain quality of your tone of voice as you say whatever you say to yourself.

Now try to consciously manufacture that exact same signal. If you are able to do this, then that signal is not reliable. To be reliable it has to be an honest expression; you must be able to tell the difference between when it is real and when you are making it happen. If you can fake it consciously and re-create it just by willing it to happen so that you cannot tell the difference, then look for another part of those experiences that you cannot consciously manufacture. It may be difficult to describe, but it will be clear to you.

This is your signal that you are congruent about what you are doing. Let it be your friend. Notice when it is there. It will be much easier to notice and pay attention to now that you know it. It is like a trusted advisor. Congruence is the signal for emotional intelligence. It is also the signal for trust.

You can also become familiar with your signal for incongruence in the same way. Incongruence is when the voices are not in harmony, when there is a wrong note somewhere, when the picture does not look quite right, when you do not yet trust the other person.

Take three instances of when you were uncertain whether to take a course of action, when something was not quite right, and go through the same procedure.

What is there in all three instances?

A feeling?
A voice tone?
A quality of the picture?

This feeling of incongruence can be your friend, stopping you from making hasty decisions that you may regret. Often we know we are incongruent, but one of our voices persuades us against our better judgement to go ahead – a triumph of wishful thinking over reality.

If you are incongruent, then the next step is to think what you need to find out in order to be congruent.

What do you need to do?
What information do you need to discover?

These signals do not mean that everything will turn out for the best. When you are congruent, you can commit yourself, you can give the situation your best. But the situation may change – once congruent does not mean always congruent.

The value of a congruence check is that it brings in all your resources, not only your intellect, conditioning and biological instincts, but also your unconscious resources. You cannot fake it and it is not under your control, therefore you have less chance of fooling yourself, confusing what you want to happen with what you fear will happen.

Now think back to a partner from the past and notice what signal is triggered by their memory.

Were you congruent?
Did you commit yourself?
Did you trust them?

Create being with this person again and notice the signal from within. It might well be a signal that was evident at the time and you chose to ignore it.

If you are in a relationship now, make the same test.

Now choose a relationship in which you got a negative signal. You need to find out what it was that made you incongruent. Maybe something was there that you were unhappy about or maybe something was missing.

To find out, first remember a time when the genetic voice was to the fore, when biological attraction was all-important.

Allow yourself to fully enter that frame of mind as you create the pictures, sounds and feelings that represent your genetic voice.

When you are fully into this mindset, think about that person again and notice your congruence and incongruence signals.

Is this signal more pronounced than when you thought of this person in general?
Does this highlight that improvement needs to be made on the level of physical attraction or is the problem somewhere else?

Now do the same exercise using the conditioned voice. Re-create this frame of mind using a time in the past calling upon what you saw, heard and felt. Again, notice your sense of what is right and what is wrong.

And if there is something wrong, notice what it might be.

Is it a belief that this other person holds that you cannot match or come to terms with?
Is this belief forcing you into a role that you do not want?

You might find that the difference is something that could be discussed and resolved now that it is identified.

Finally, go into the frame of mind and physiology that represents you being at your most logical. Become common sense personified and look at that other person. With the information you have gathered from the other two voices you can trust your sense and signals for what is right and wrong to tell you how this relationship will be for you. Your intelligence will tell you what is needed to make you happy.

---

You can apply these ideas to any part of your relationship. I (Robin) recently bought a house with my wife. When we decided to move we sat down with a map of the country and chose a number of areas that we thought might be suitable. They were the areas that met our criteria for accessibility to work, friends and family, for the availability of open spaces and the sea, for the quality of schooling and for the price of property. This process was dominated by our intellect.

Then we spent weekends in some of the areas to see whether they felt right to us. This was very much a process of noticing our internal signals about familiarity, the way we would fit in with the community, how happy people looked and how 'at home' places felt. Communities and areas give off an aura about the shared beliefs and values that are dominant. People attracted to live in the Midlands had a different set of beliefs and values from people who lived in Cornwall, and a very different sense of who they were.

Having sorted for area through our conditioned voice, we then brought our intellect back into the equation by getting specific about what we could afford, what features a new house would need to have for us, where it should be located in relation to the amenities, what travelling would be like and how much maintenance would be necessary.

We then viewed some properties. Upon arriving at one I knew immediately if it was wrong. I knew as soon as a house 'looked back at me' whether or not it had echoes of the past and familiarity that made me warm to it. My wife had similar (though not identical) internal messages. Then we went inside some of the houses. It was at this point that my genetic voice and my conditioning started to wrestle with each other. Although I did not know it at the time, my basic drives were surveying the territory the house occupied to check on its security, which was important as we had young children. Was it overlooked? Was it exposed? Was it defensible? These criteria overruled the conditioned voice's sense of comfort. My wife was checking the garden to see if it was a safe place for the children to play in. Was the kitchen clean? Was the bathroom hygienic? Were the bedrooms close together for speed of access should anything go wrong in the night?

Having gathered information we went away and our intelligence came back into the discussion. We made sure that our genetic voices and our conditioning were taken into account once we found a property that met the criteria laid down by our shared common sense. There were times when other voices interrupted and stated their case: 'Yes, I know it's near a main road but it just felt so comfortable to me' or 'I know it's a long way from the school, but think what we could do with that garden.' In relationships, the intellectual voice is best used to understand and accommodate the other two and to take a calm, calculated view of what is likely to happen. The intellectual voice is good for working out the consequences of something. When emotion and logic clash, emotion will usually prevail. The intellect needs to inform emotion, not try to override it, and it deserves the chance to speak out on every relationship you enter into.

My wife and I (Robin) engage our intellectual voices every month for a meeting that we run on business lines. We have an agenda covering our home, the children, the time we spend together, our outcomes, plans and objectives, and our finances, with plenty of room for any other business. It can be a bit dry at times, but it does keep us in touch with each other. We know where we are and this helps us feel more together.

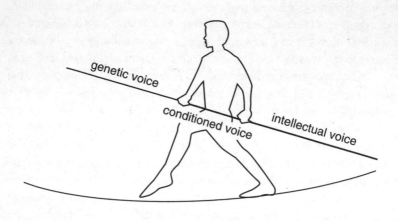

Intelligent harmony

# 5

# The Relationship You Want

## WHAT DO I WANT?

■ This is the question that keeps you searching for a good relationship or trying to improve the one you are in. Whatever we have, we can imagine making it better. We all wake in the morning with some purpose, however humdrum, and it is not likely to be 'How can I have a really unhappy day today?'

You may not be sure exactly what you want in a relationship. You may have a vague sense of dissatisfaction about your life. Perhaps you do not have a partner and want one. Perhaps you see other people in happy relationships and wonder how they do it. Perhaps you and your partner are caught in a cycle of blame and frustration with each other. You have both forgotten or now take for granted the magic that once brought you together. You want something, something better than you have at the moment.

When you are in a relationship shared goals are important. People can live together for years without realizing that they want very different things from their relationship. We take these life choices and directions for granted and instead become preoccupied with the smaller goals like where we should go on holiday – which often reflect the great difference in partners' goals and what they want from life and their relationship.

Holidays are a perfect example of values and beliefs in action that may lead to disagreement and anger between partners. We all want holidays, we want to go somewhere different, to do something different. The one thing that all holidays have in common is that they take you out of your normal life. But where to? Holidays rank high in the stress charts and many people haul themselves back exhausted from the break that they so looked forward to, glad to rejoin 'normal' life.

We think that the ultimate compatibility test for a couple is to first of all agree on a holiday, then go on it together, have a good time and finally both be glad that they went. Holidays are the best area in which to test out your partner's beliefs and values. For example, one partner wants a relaxing holiday by the beach. Lying in the sun being waited on is their idea of heaven. The other partner would get bored out of their skull by this. They would prefer an adventure safari trek. The way you both make your decisions will tell you a lot about your communication style and flexibility. We know couples that solve this perennial problem in different ways. In one case the husband decides one year and his wife the next. With another couple, she decides, he agrees. A third couple fights every year about it and comes to an unhappy compromise which neither of them fully enjoys. A fourth takes separate holidays (they have no children). These choices highlight how they decide everyday matters in their relationship.

What do you want in a relationship? Sometimes we are reluctant to think about relationships and affairs of the heart like this, as if they should be completely spontaneous and having any sort of goal would be cheating. To this, we reply, everything you do is directed towards some goal – even sitting or standing where you are, reading this book and the small movements of your body as you read. They all achieve something. In a little while you will put the book down and move on to doing something else, in other words, trying to achieve what you want next. We always act with purpose, we cannot help it. The clearer you can be about it, the more likely you are to achieve it. Otherwise you might as well say, 'Actually I don't care what relationship I have, I do not care what sort of partner I end up with, it's all the same to me.' But we don't do that. We want satisfaction. We do not purposely go on a date from hell where everything goes wrong.

Sometimes people are reluctant to set goals in their personal relationships because it seems like tempting fate. They believe that once you let on that you want something, then the world will hold it from you like a mean parent who delights in frustrating you. We have one friend who shuns any sort of goal setting for just that reason. His parents rewarded him for restraint, for politeness, for the absence of desire. When he was too eager for something as a child, his parents would not give it to him. ' "I want" does not get' was their mantra. No wonder he avoids setting goals.

Goals *do* belong in relationships, first as a way of making clear what you want as an individual, secondly to make clear what you want as a couple, and thirdly as a way of problem solving, where to set a goal is to point to the way out of a bad situation.

## What Do You Want in a Relationship?

There are a few guidelines here. The first is make sure you think in the positive – what you do want, not what you do not want. When we asked one acquaintance what they wanted in a relationship she said, 'I don't want anyone like my last boyfriend, arrogant little uncaring creep. I don't know what I saw in him.' She was quite clear what she did not want, but that did not help her at all to get what she wanted. We didn't think that she picked her last boyfriend by saying to herself, 'Here's an arrogant little creep who looks like he won't care. Let's go out with him and have a bad time. I've had much too much fun lately.' Unless she is clear what she really does want, she might find herself with another equally unsuitable partner, but in a different way.

This is what happens when someone jumps to another partner on the rebound. They often pick someone who is as far removed from their last partner as possible. Unfortunately, this new partner will have all the opposite vices. When you choose partners on the rebound, you are liable to get a variety of vices, but no nearer to what you really want. So make sure you think about what you want, not what you want to avoid. There are as many unsuitable partners in the world as there are suitable ones and to specify what you do not want in detail would take forever. Life is too short to find a good relationship completely by trial and error. So if you find yourself describing the sort of relationship you do not want, ask yourself, 'If I don't have that, what do I want instead?' or 'If I don't make that mistake again, what will I do?'

Thinking positive is not Pollyanna optimism, although optimism is just as realistic as pessimism. With the future unformed, it's what you do right now that counts. We tend to head towards what we think about. We are drawn towards and often get it. Ask any tennis player what happens if they whisper to themselves on a crucial point, 'I must not net this one.' What are they thinking of? Netting the ball. What image is in their mind? Hitting the ball into the net. And what often happens? Their brain forgets about the 'not' and just hears 'hit ... net' and then they curse their bad skill. It's not their skill that is at fault, but their way of thinking.

We are at the mercy of a stream of negatives from early childhood. 'Don't do this...' 'Don't do that...' 'Don't touch...' There is research that suggests that in Western European cultures a child will hear nine negative commands for every positive one. So we grow up adept at knowing what not to do, but sometimes at a loss about knowing what to do instead. This also means that the conditioned voice is made up mostly of negatives, which is why it can be unduly constricting. We are not taught to be good citizens, but taught how not to be bad ones.

The second question to ask about your goals is: 'How will I know that I am getting what I want?' Positive evidence is best.

There can never be any final evidence that you have the relationship of your dreams, because both you and your partner change, so you have to keep working. Every day you have to create the relationship you want by building on what you have. You create a good relationship, you do not fall into it like falling asleep. However, there will be some signposts on the road that let you know that you are heading in the right direction.

Examples of positive evidence would be:

'I will feel great after being with them, they will be attentive and listen to what I say.'
'They will take care with their appearance.'
'They will be a fantastic lover.'

You might also have some negatives here, too, for example:

'I won't be hanging around the telephone all evening waiting for them to ring when they said they would.'
'I won't be paying for all the meals.'
'I won't have to apologize afterwards for him to my friends.'

Next you need to think of the qualities you have that will help you get the relationship you want:

Do you have enough money to go to the places you want?
Do you have a wide social circle of friends?

Do you have any role models? Perhaps you have some friends who are successful in the way that you want to be. How do they do it?

We are not talking about copying people. There may be small actions that they do that you could copy, but usually success in relationships is more about the sort of qualities you have and your beliefs about yourself, the world and the opposite sex.

We have already looked at beliefs and values in detail. There is a strange belief that is very common for men – that to ask for help or even to admit to needing any help or guidance in creating a good relationship makes you a failure. There are men who would rather be dragged backwards naked through a hedge than admit that they might not be God's gift to women and know all about the dating and relationship game. They would rather be caught reading *Playboy* than relationship self-help books. This belief may come as part of the conditioned voice, either from family or school. It is a self-defeating belief because extreme self-reliance does not usually make for a good relationship – but rather one that will benefit from help!

## TIME AND ATTENTION

There are two great resources that you already have that you will need to make a great relationship. Both are completely under your control and we all have them in the same quantity. They are time and attention.

Are you prepared to give time to a relationship? How does it fit with your lifestyle? Will you give the other person the attention they deserve?

Most relationships deteriorate and may eventually fail not with a bang but with a whimper – they wither through lack of time and attention, like neglected flowers, because one or both partners withdraws their time and attention. Attention is what makes us come alive; it brings out the best in us. We all recognize a good listener is what makes a good talker. We feel good with such people, that is why they are so popular, not necessarily because they are full of witty repartee, but because they make the person they are with feel valued and good about themselves.

What is the most fascinating topic in the world? What is the most immediate and important subject that you can never have enough of?

What is the topic that you spend most of your life thinking about, talking about and paying attention to?

You.

You are the most important topic to yourself. So anyone who pays attention and listens to you automatically makes you feel good. They are interested in what is most important to you.

## How Do You Pay Attention?

There are two ways – one that you can do and one that you can be.

What you can do is match the other person in important respects – match eye contact, match height so you are on the same level, so, for example, you are not standing while the other person is sitting. Match closeness. How close is comfortable? Match your voice so that you do not speak much more quickly or slowly than the other person. Do not try to match exactly; it is more important to avoid badly mismatching another person and making them feel ill at ease.

Carrying on a conversation with someone who talks a great deal more quickly or loudly than you do, for example, is a little off-putting. It is also awkward to talk to someone who does not match eye contact. Eye contact in itself is not necessarily good or bad. Some people like a lot of eye contact and give a lot. Others are shyer and do not give as much. However, as people become more intimate they tend to give more eye contact and for longer periods.

Matching tends to make people feel at ease with each other. People tend to like people who are like themselves and the way they judge this is by whether they feel at ease with them. Most people who get on well with people match their partners. Look around in restaurants, parks, bars, anywhere people are talking together. You will be able to tell which people are at ease by whether they match each other's body language. It works like a dance. Good dancers complement the other person's movements, in fact it is impossible to see who is leading and who is following, and a good relationship has that quality too. Dancing partners do not exactly mimic each other's movements because then they would tread on each other's toes. (In fact if you want to make someone feel really uncomfortable, try and mimic them. When they notice they will become very uneasy.) Done with respect, however, matching is an honest attempt to understand the other person's world by being like them in a small way.

In conversation we all match people to some extent and we are not usually aware of it. The stronger and deeper the relationship, the closer the matching. Lovers will often be breathing in unison, so closely are they immersed in each other. Simple matching can put you both at ease, but it is only a beginning. Matching is evidence of a good relationship and while it can help at the outset if you do it consciously, it will not by itself create trust or rapport. Trust is created over time by being dependable.

Matching works to help others feel at ease. Mismatching works if you want to break a conversation. If you have guests who will not go home, how do you deal with the situation? Many people will simply say that it's time for bed. Others will break any form of matching that has taken place. They might stand up, stretch and change the quality or volume of their voice. We knew one instance where the husband got tired of the genteel mismatching that he and his wife were doing. It was not working and their guests were embarking on another tedious anecdote. He excused himself for a moment and went into the bedroom, where he changed into his pyjamas. Then he came back in the room and sat down as if nothing had happened. His guests left almost immediately, funnily enough without remarking on his change of clothes. We guess they got the message.

---

Think back to a time when you were having a discussion with someone close and you were in disagreement. Also, make the time one where you were determined not to be wrong, to stand your ground or to make the other person feel bad about themselves. Were you deliberately trying to mismatch in any way? Were you changing your posture if the other person shifted to match yours? Did you change the quality of your voice or avoid eye contact? You cannot fake trust by mimicking body posture, but you can break it if you constantly mismatch.

Now think back to a time when you may have been attracted to someone at a distance, in a pub or at a party, but where once you began to speak to them you realized there would not be common ground. Remember how you may have unknowingly tried to match them in order to build rapport. Remember how you may have mismatched them in order to move away.

Very few situations are best resolved or improved from a position of mismatching, unless you want to break a contact. I (Joseph) sometimes overhear my 17-year-old daughter on the telephone. She may talk for a long time, but I can always tell when she wants to stop. She starts talking more quickly and slightly more loudly. Ten seconds later, she will say something like, 'Well, I really must go now...' Mismatching has its place and it can be useful.

Apart from matching, the other way to give another person attention is far more powerful – you become intensely interested in them. When you do this you will match them automatically at the right level without having to think about it. You will want to know:

What are they like?
What sort of person are they?
How deep do they go?
What have they done in their life?
How can they possibly think what they think?
What is important to them?

Imagine, if you will, that this other person has done all the things you want to do, knows what you want to know and has the secret to making you happy if only you can find it. People are only boring if we do not dig beneath surface appearances. No one is boring, they only appear boring if they have not met anyone who is capable of finding out what they are really like. There are no boring people, only bored listeners.

## WHAT STOPS YOU?

Continuing with the questions to clarify your goals, you need to ask what stops you having the sort of relationship you want right away. Assume for this exercise that every barrier is something that is within your power to overcome. Some will need you to re-examine your beliefs. Some may involve learning new skills. Make sure every objection you find is put in a form that *you* can act on, that does not mean you are weak or to blame. Unless you put the barriers in those terms they will not be surmountable.

For example, you may have the objection: 'No one wants to talk to me at parties.' If this were literally true then that would be the end of the matter. Your romantic life would be over before it had begun. Luckily, it cannot be literally true. It is a generalization. Secondly, it is mind reading. To do something about it, you need to turn it into something you can influence. Take out any reference to what other people want or what you are forced to do. Just restate the difficulty in terms of what happens.

You might change it first of all to: 'When I am at parties, people do not talk to me.'

Then change that into something that is about you, so you can do something about it: 'I make it difficult for people to talk to me.'

Now this is within your power to change and you can start to see why it might be so and what you can do about it. Remember, this does *not* make you at fault. It puts it in such a way that it is under *your* control.

When you think about the problems in this way, you can turn them into further goals, treat them as beliefs and decide if they are really the barriers they appear to be.

The following exercise leads on from this.

---

Look at the wider consequences of what you want.

What would change in your life if you got what you wanted?
What would you have to do that you do not do now?
Who else might be affected?

Think about what advantage there is in the present situation. However unsatisfactory, there is always some advantage, otherwise you would have changed it by now. Sometimes we resist change because of fear of the unknown. Think about what you would lose if you got what you wanted. How can you keep the advantages of the present situation?

Lastly, does this goal fit in with your sense of self? Does it feel right to you?

---

## Changing Other People

Beware of trying to change your partner. So many people see the problems of others and forget that any relationship problem is a shared problem. It reminds us of the joke about the experienced pilot who was training a new co-pilot in an unfamiliar plane. At 20,000 feet they heard a sudden horrible crunching sound and one of the engines started to disintegrate. As if this wasn't enough, they saw one of the landing wheels fall off. The pilot struggled to gain control as the plane started to judder.

'Boy,' said the new co-pilot, 'have *you* got a problem!'

Most of us know that change is almost impossible without the will to change. However, there may be some scope in asking the question 'What can you do that might make them *want* to make that change?' Often we try to argue people into a change, forgetting that rational argument is not at all motivating. Very few people will say, 'Yes, you're absolutely right. I see I have been mistaken and I will change. Just tell me how.' Logic never convinces anyone, unless there are two conditions. The first is that everyone agrees to accept the rules of logic. The second is that no emotions are involved. How many times do those conditions hold in personal relationships? Never. Men particularly overrate the power of reason and logic. It is not that emotional is unreasonable; it just does not obey the same laws. It doesn't play the same game.

The way to deal with changing another person is to make it so that they really want to change, that they feel happier for doing it, in accordance with *their* values. This can be tricky. What of those people who keep saying they will change but never do? You have several choices. You can accept them for what they are if this fits your values. You can leave them if what they do is bad enough to warrant it. Usually, however, the situation where they say they will change but do not means two things. First they are agreeing with you to pacify you and secondly they are happier as they are now – the present situation has an advantage they do not want to give up. Nagging does not usually help, especially with those people (often men) who do not like to feel pressured into a change. All you can do is to make it really clear what matters to you and try to find out what it is about the present situation that makes it attractive to them. If you can both find a way whereby they can keep that advantage in another way, then they will change. Otherwise support and reinforce any change that does happen – even the slightest. Sometimes a change 'trade off' works – trade one change they want you to make for one change you want them to make.

## BLAME

Setting goals is very useful for solving relationship problems as well, because a goal is 'what you want different'. When you are clear what that is, you have a way out of the problem.

In a sense we have problems all the time when we do not have what we want to have, but they only register when our dissatisfaction reaches a certain critical level. Then we want to change.

Just like physical pain, people have different thresholds. One person will flee a relationship the moment they get the slightest hint that the other person is making decisions for them or telling them what to do. Others will be happy living in the other person's pocket, letting them run their life for them.

With a relationship problem, there is another person to focus on and we tend not to think in terms of goals but of blame. We focus not on what we want but on what is wrong and who is at fault.

Many people go through a cycle with relationships:

First they enjoy them, get great pleasure from them and thank their lucky stars they have them.

Then they settle into a comfortable acceptance of what they have. The initial thrill has worn off. They do not put any attention into keeping that pleasure, but become accustomed to it. They do not know how to make it different.

Then even that drains away and they become dissatisfied. They do not know how to recapture the original joy or how to create new joy.

Then they reach a threshold where the situation becomes intolerable and they resolve to do something about it. At this point blame enters the scene in a big way.

In the main our culture focuses on what is wrong; it's remedial, not preventative. There are far more counsellors and therapists to help unhappy couples than there are agencies teaching people how to live together happily. Both counselling and medicine lean towards making good what has gone bad. Prevention still comes a poor second to fixing what has already gone wrong. We wonder what a health service would be like if it were modelled on the service in ancient China. There, doctors were only paid as long as their patients remained well. When the patients fell ill, the doctors were not paid until the patient got better. This is rather more motivating than our present system, where the medical profession gets more money the more people are ill. Perhaps relationship counsellors should only be paid if the people they see have a happy relationship.

Couples tend to talk most when there is a breakdown or a problem to solve. Our preoccupation is often to apportion blame, vent our anger and wallow in the negative consequences of what has happened. Arguments develop like tennis matches – hitting the blame back to each other. One couple we knew ran their lives together like a competition. They counted blame points against each other, which they could cash in later for a free mistake. The balance of power went backwards and forwards depending who was most in debt to the other by being at fault more times or more seriously. They had a sophisticated scoring system that was never discussed, but both seemed to share it and were bound by it.

The shadow of blame

---

Here is a little exercise to get a sense of what blame can do to you. Take something that has gone wrong between you and your partner. Make it something that has little significance. You can move on to the life and death stuff later.

Here are six questions for you to answer that assumes someone is to blame. Make sure you ask them in an accusatory tonality like a prosecution lawyer.

What exactly is the problem with you?
And just how long has this been a problem for you?
Who or what are you blaming for this?
How bad is this?
How does it make you feel?
Why haven't you sorted this out yet?

These questions are likely to make you feel uncomfortable and do nothing to solve the problem. Blame is often a ghastly game of pass the parcel. Couples have arguments that essentially go round and round like this:

'It's your fault...'
'No it's not, it's yours...'
'But if you hadn't done that...'
'But I would never had done that if you hadn't...'

Nothing is solved. No wonder after a while they give up and suffer in silence. Rather than settle differences, this type of conversation only tries to settle who is to blame.

You have probably noticed how easy it would be to expand on the six blameworthy questions. Now, shake yourself free of any bad feeling they may have generated and think about the same problem again but with these questions:

What do I want instead?
How will I feel when I have that?
What else will improve when that happens?
Of all the resources I have, which ones will be particularly useful in helping me solve this problem?

When did I succeed with something like this before?
What is the first step I can take to change this situation in the way I want?

These are more empowering questions, they focus on change, on what you want, and make you feel better as well as motivating you towards solving the problem. They are the sort of questions to ask yourself when you have a problem (that is, some situation you do not want) and to help your partner deal with their problems when you talk about them together.

You can also look at problems you have together, simply replacing 'I' with 'we':

What do we want?
How will we feel when we have that?
What else will improve when that happens?
What resources do we have that will help us to get what we want?
When did we succeed in solving something like this before?
What practical steps can we take right now that will help us move towards what we want?

Blame sets you against the other. These questions bring you together to search for a solution.

---

Your goals as a couple are important, too. Having joint goals and objectives, and helping each other achieve individual or personal goals help make relationships work. Teamwork is based on a common approach to shared aims. Whether it is planning a holiday, buying a house, starting a family or organizing dinner, the more involved both parties can be, the greater the bond between them.

I (Robin) knew one couple whose only area of compatibility was decorating their house. They would choose a room, agree on a colour scheme, buy the paint and paper, strip the old décor off, prepare for the new and carry out the work together. Then they would get people in to look at their handywork and admire it. No sooner were their hands washed clean of paint then they would choose another room and the process would begin again. They were as happy as it was possible to be, even though they never spoke of anything other than decoration to me. It was all they needed.

It has been said (mostly by men) that behind every great man there is a woman. It would be better to say that behind every great person there is probably a supportive partner. Most of us feel better about ourselves when we achieve what we want to achieve. It does wonders for our self-image and confidence. When a partner helps us achieve what we want it increases our bond with them because they support us. However, support should be mutual. If one partner becomes a tool or resource to help the other and gets nothing back in return then this will lead to resentment.

We heard a well-known retailer being interviewed on radio. When asked how his family felt about the time he spent at work and the effort they had to put in to support him, he initially went silent. Then he said that he was only achieving for them. They wanted the head of the household to be a prominent figure. 'Anyway,' he added faintly, 'I think they do.'

## WHAT DO WE WANT?

When you are working with your partner on what you want as a couple, you can use the same questions that you used earlier to work out what you wanted. With these questions, a joint session on what you want need not be a prelude to an argument! These questions will clarify what you want and so make it easier to achieve.

By the emphasis you place on different parts of the process you can plan to achieve one off goals, such as buying a new house, or long-term changes in your relationship, such as getting closer, having more fun or spending more time together. It is a flexible process that benefits from practice.

Here are the questions for shared goals.

What do we want?
Make sure you answer this in positive terms. There will be plenty of things you do not want, but think what you do want instead. If it is to stop arguing so frequently, then say, 'We'd like to live in a more peaceful environment,' so that your mind is not constantly creating pictures of arguments.

Once you have a shared description of what you want you can then increase your motivation by looking at the benefits beyond the change. All you do here is ask the question: 'When we've got that, what will that give us?' The answer may run as follows:

'We'd like to live in a peaceful environment.
That will enable us to relax more and feel more rested.
That will make home a better place to come home to.
That will help build our relationship.
We will feel happier and enjoy life more.'

Next, how you will know you are achieving what you want? What will change and how?

It is best to have a clear sensory-specific description of what success will look, feel, sound, smell and taste like. You will then know exactly what signs and behaviour to seek out as evidence of achievement. By having this description you create an awareness of the desired future and will make it more real. For instance, if your goal is to be a better parent, then that concept will remain fuzzy and ill-defined unless you can state specifically that you will be spending a definable amount of time with your children involving them in specific activities. When stating your evidence, describe the results in terms of both what you will see, hear and feel and what others will see, hear and feel.

Next, make a list of your resources. Do you have the resources necessary to help you get what you both want?

This will include personal qualities, possessions, money and role models, as previously discussed in relation to personal goals *(see p. 106)*. Then think what you will have to give up in order to get what you want.

A couple I (Robin) worked with on this process were about to receive a substantial redundancy package. They had their minds set on buying and running a country pub. It had been their dream for years. When we reached this stage and asked if there was anything they would have to give up in pursuit of their outcome, a whole list of hobbies and pastimes came forth that needed to be sacrificed on this altar of achievement. They would have no time for golf, tennis, their many friends or their dogs. This list went on and on. Although the pub had been their dream for many years, they now realized it was impractical and the loss of their other pleasures would surely have brought pressure to bear on their relationship.

Remember that the present situation will have advantages that you may lose and these are not always obvious. Another couple I worked with were both desperate for the man to become more demonstrative and loving. He tried to force his arms to leave his sides and embrace his wife, but they would not move. He tried to look her in the face and smile, but he could not. We went down the route of looking at what he would have to give up if he became more loving and finally discovered his desire to be true to his father, who was even more undemonstrative than he was. Being demonstrative for this man meant denying his love for his father. Not to copy his father would have meant, in the son's view of the world, that he was being critical of his father and rejecting his love. What we were able to do was logically discuss other ways in which the son could be true to his father. We were then able to incorporate those ways into new behaviour. Then he was free to show affection to his wife.

Now ask, 'Does our goal feel right for us individually and together?'

Any wavering here indicates you need to review your goal in some way, because you are not totally committed. Part of you may be, but another part may not be.

Then you need to plan and think what you can do directly to achieve what you want.

Goals do not usually drop into your lap without effort. To pursue a goal over which you have little control is not only soul destroying, but tends to lead to early resignation. Identify the obstacles and start the process using small, easily achievable goals over which you have complete control and influence to establish a winning pattern.

There are two ways you can approach these shared goals. Some people prefer to start from where they are and plan towards the goal. Some like to work backwards. If you are forward planners, a useful question to ask yourselves is, 'What's stopping you?' For example, if your outcome is to buy a bigger house and you ask the question 'What's stopping you?', the answer might be, 'We don't know where we want to live.' Consequently, choosing where to live would be the first step in your plan. If you then ask, 'When we've chosen where to live what's stopping us buying a bigger house?' the response to that becomes the next step in your plan.

If you prefer to plan backwards, your questioning process should start with the words, 'What would come immediately before...?' With a goal of buying a bigger house what would come immediately before moving in would be organizing the move. And what would come immediately before that would be exchanging contracts, etc.

One of the dangers of working on goals is that your personal goals may clash with the shared goals. However they do not have to be exclusive and it is important to be honest about how your shared goals fit in with your own plans. When you work on personal goals you need to be aware of this and consider how your partner will be affected. Shared goals must come before personal goals, because there are two of you agreeing them.

There are two dangers here. One is if your relationship takes a poor second place to your own wishes, needs and desires, your partner may end up feeling like a fashion accessory. The second danger is when you lose your own individual identity in the relationship and you do everything together, agree on everything and do not have any separate life apart from each other, but form a sort of merged personality.

A good relationship is one where the people are close enough to give each other the space they need. And when you give your partner space, you create some for yourself as well. You need balance. There are no absolutes about having a great relationship, the rules change just when you think you have got the hang of them. But being in a good relationship should make you more of a person; it should allow you to express yourself more fully, not less. If you give up too much of yourself in favour of your partnership, you are likely to feel resentful and unhappy.

On the other hand, a relationship must be more than just a way of taking care of your own material and sexual needs while you get on and do exactly what you always intended to do anyway. We know some couples whose relationship got better when one of the partners asserted themselves more than before. There have been other couples, of course, where one partner needed to be less assertive, to pay more attention to what their partner wanted and to start to build a genuine partnership.

Whatever you need to do to balance your relationship, you have to stop doing it when you reach a healthy balance again. Think of your relationship as a balance between your wants and needs, your partner's wants and needs, and your shared goals.

With one couple I (Joseph) knew, the man, who had been previously very passive, asserted himself more but then went too far, leaving his wife feeling not only surprised but also bewildered and resentful. Then he had to retreat, which was highly confusing for him at first because it seemed as if he had been wrong to change. 'But that was what I *was* doing!' he said. 'And we agreed it was wrong!' But it was not wrong for him to make that change, he just overdid it.

A good relationship is about keeping a balance and the right thing to do is what puts you both back in balance. The right thing to do one year may be precisely the wrong thing to do the next, which is why relationships are the most wonderful as well as the most confusing areas of life.

# 6

# Change

■ Now we have talked about what you want, we can talk about change.

When you think about change, remember there are two aspects. One is keeping what is good about the present. Whenever we think of change, we often lose sight of what has to stay the same for that change to be effective. No one changes everything all at once. The second is replacing what you do not want with something better. Changing the way that you act in relationships is going to bring you some benefit, or you would not bother. But that does not make where you are now a bad place to be. Wanting to change does not negate everything that has gone before. You do not have to see the past as a waste in order to make the future better. Staying the same in order to validate how you have been previously is one of the most limiting beliefs that exists.

Although we focus on individual change, really there is no such thing. When you are in a relationship you both have to change. If you change, the other person has to change as well to accommodate what you are doing differently. It may only be a slight change, but it will be necessary. So both partners will change, although one may start the process.

This means that if you want to change something in a relationship and you resolve to be different, your partner must support you. They must make it easy for you to make the change by reinforcing and supporting what you both want. We have seen many examples where one partner wants to change because what they are doing is not working. They try, but the other partner acts just as they always did. This makes it very difficult for the first partner to change.

You will have an idea of how your conditioning is limiting you and maybe preventing you from doing what you want to do, what you feel would be worthwhile and positive. It might be that you are drawn to certain types of people, all of whom turn out to be unhelpful and damaging to you. You wonder how you found them when you were not looking for them. It might be that you have a way of destroying relationships just when they are becoming positive and fulfilling. It might be that you are able to avoid meeting anybody at all. You will have a sense that if something were different about yourself then the relationships in your life would change for the better.

Other people are always offering advice and most of it we ignore. To pay attention would mean that there is something wrong with us and that is not a comfortable idea. They must be wrong. No one changes just because others tell them to, they must be convinced themselves that it is worthwhile. However, if many people tell you the same thing, then you need to sit up and pay attention. This is very direct feedback. Others will not be so direct, they will just stop seeing you!

When you think about what to change, consider the weight of evidence. Ignoring it is foolish. It reminds us of the man who walks into a tailor's shop and asks to look at red check material. The proprietor gets angry. 'You're the eighth person this morning wanting red check and I'm fed up with saying we do not stock red check because there's no call for it.'

Think about what people have said about you that they perceived as negative. Notice how many people have said the same thing. If you have received repeated feedback about the way you are and how you influence others just consider whether there might be some substance in what is said. You do not have to agree with it, just consider the possibility. Repeated feedback indicates a shared perception. Perhaps your view of the world might benefit from adjustment.

## THE RELATIONSHIP QUESTION

How satisfied are you with your relationship at the moment? If you had a magic wand that would allow you to make any change you wanted in the way you form relationships, what would it be?

Perhaps you are in a good relationship and want to make it better. But perhaps you have found yourself caught in a pattern of unsatisfactory relationships. You recognize it after a while, stop the relationship, move on, start again with someone new, only to find that when you get to know them, they have the same faults as your last partner. This is because a relationship is the answer to a question. We tend to have a question that we seek to answer by finding a partner we can love and who will love us.

This question usually comes from our upbringing and is embedded deep in the conditioned voice. It may come from the way that our parents brought us up, it may come from more general experiences. When we are children we want to know how the world works. We want it to make sense. We want our parents' relationship to make sense. This leaves us with some questions that we try to live out the answer to, because we were never able to ask them in words at the time. The answer to your basic relationship question is what you are trying to find out when you enter a close relationship.

Here are some examples of this question that we have found:

Am I lovable?
Can men and women live together without fighting?
Do people like me?
What happens if people quarrel?
Is love possible?
Can I be faithful to one person?
How important are good looks in a partner?
Am I interesting enough to engage someone as a partner?
Are other people interesting enough?
Are relationships possible without violence?
Do I have to marry to be happy?
How soon can I have sexual intercourse after meeting a person for the first time?
Can I find my soulmate?
Will this person be acceptable to my parents?
How can I be happy?
How can I make another person happy?
Can this person handle my moods?

Your basic relationship question deeply influences how you approach relationships. Other people will pick it up, usually unconsciously. I (Joseph) knew one woman who had a number of relationships; none worked for more than a year. She felt that all were vaguely unsatisfactory, but could not really say why. She was frustrated that none of her relationships really flowered into anything more than passing alliances. When she explored this state of affairs, she realized that she would drift out of relationships because none of the men seemed to be good enough. She was always left with the nagging idea that there was someone else out there who was better. When she thought more deeply about her upbringing, she made some connections. The relationship question she was trying to answer was: 'Are you good enough for me?'

She had been brought up by a doting father who used to say, 'Nothing is too good for you' (which is an interesting ambiguous phrase if you take it literally). He would only allow her the very best of everything. As she grew older she expected the best and would apply the same test to a boyfriend as she applied to cars, clothes, food and household objects – the slightest imperfection and they were taken back to the shop to be exchanged. The way she had been brought up had made her too much of a perfectionist about other people. Behind her initial question was another question: 'What's wrong with you?' It was as if she assumed that everyone had their faults and flaws (she was right about that), but once she had found out what they were, the person was rejected.

There was a positive side to the initial question that was important to keep    she deserved the best. Her father had taught her that she was important and worthy of the best. This gave her tremendous self-esteem and she was very popular. People with high self-esteem are a delight to be with; they do not have to prove anything to themselves and they do not try to make you anything you are not. When the woman realized this, she changed her question to: 'How can I bring out the best in my partner?'

Here is an exercise you can use to explore your own relationship question.

---

Think of the romantic relationships that you have been in.

What did they have in common?
Is there a pattern?

What typically goes wrong?

If you had one question you could ask any prospective partner, what would it be?

If a relationship does go wrong, what question does it answer? (You might catch yourself saying something like, 'I knew it wouldn't work out because...')

What are you trying to find out about the other person?

What are you trying to find out about yourself?

What was missing from that relationship? (Whatever it was, your question may be how you can find it.)

Relationship questions need not be a problem, they can be very helpful. It depends how you live out the answer or make your partner live out the answer.

When you have found a question that seems to be important to you, look at it more closely. What is assumed in the question?

The assumption may be perfectly reasonable, but it may also have hidden depths. For example the question, 'Would this person be acceptable to my parents?' assumes a number of things – first that it is important that *your* partner meets your *parents'* values; secondly, that you know what your parents' values are.

The question, 'Is love possible?' implies a doubt, otherwise why would you be asking the question?

When you find your question, pay attention to the voice tone that you use when you ask it. For example, the question, 'Am I lovable?' could have an element of slight doubt or total incredulity, depending on the voice tone that you use to ask it.

Look at your question and see whether it is open or closed. A closed question can be answered by 'yes' or 'no'. For example, 'Am I lovable?' is a closed question. It is certainly a very important question and a lot depends on what sort of evidence you will accept. An open question is one that cannot be answered by a simple 'yes' or 'no'. 'How lovable am I?' would be an example.

In general, an open question is much better than a closed one. It invites more exploration, more ways of acting to get answers, and has fewer hidden assumptions. A closed question can be answered by 'no'; and this leaves you with nowhere to go.

If your question is a closed one, turning it into an open one will be a step forward. For example:

'Can I find my soulmate?' becomes 'What sort of person would be my soulmate?'
'Will this person be acceptable to my parents?' becomes 'How important is it for a partner to be acceptable to my parents?'
'Can I make them happy?' becomes 'How can I make them happy?'
'Can this person handle my moods?' becomes 'How well can they handle my moods?'

Now take a look at the question and see what sort of values are behind it. How important are the values to you?
   For example, 'Will this person protect me?' contains the value of safety. 'Can I have a good time with this person?' has the value of fun. Finally, what does your question tell you about the sort of person you are?
   It will tell you a lot about your values, beliefs and what you assume about yourself and others. Couples often come together when their two questions match each other, both having the same values and the same assumptions. Sometimes the questions complement each other if one supplies a value the other is looking for.

---

## WHAT WE DO AND WHAT WE MEAN

A friend of ours was constantly defending himself against accusations of selfishness. He would argue vehemently that he was generous. He knew he was generous. That is, he knew he wanted to be generous and he would be, as soon as he had enough money. It is interesting because for him 'being generous' meant giving out money. Yet if you think of your experience with people, you do not judge generosity only by what they do with money. It is possible to be generous of spirit, giving of yourself. We both know people who have very little money, yet are generous with their time and their attention and often with what money they have. Time and attention are more valuable than money and we all have them in abundance.
   The second interesting fact about our friend is that he is judging himself by his intentions and not by his behaviour. We all tend to have double standards like this. We know that we are trying to do well, or would if we could. If things turn out badly, then we made a mistake, but

we know what we were trying to achieve and this carries the greater weight in our reality. Yet we tend to judge others by the results. Their intentions are invisible to us. We also tend to take things personally and blame people when what they do hurts us. Yet very seldom do they intend to cause us pain.

There are some people who – consciously or not – feel they are unworthy of their partner. They often hurt their partner to make them leave in order to reinforce their own sense of inadequacy. They hurt their partner as a roundabout way of hurting themselves. The way out of this unhappy situation for them is to look closely at their beliefs and values about relationships and perhaps work out their basic relationship question. Such a limiting belief is often embedded in the conditioned voice saying something like 'You are not a worthy partner for anyone. Anyone who gets into a relationship with you is doing you a favour.'

Whenever you judge any action, whether it is yours or another's, remember there are always two sides. There is what it looks like from the inside – the intention – and what it looks like from the outside – the result. The intention is invisible from the outside. Putting ourselves in another person's shoes can help us be more forgiving, as we can see their action from both sides before judging them or reacting hastily to what they do.

Think on this example. One of the partners in a family with three growing children takes on the role of breadwinner. Let's say it is the father. To keep his job and secure a sufficient income he has to work long hours, show emotional commitment, pay a high personal price in terms of stress and fatigue and finish each day having little time and energy left for his family. To make his time at work more palatable and because he has an aptitude for his job, he chooses to like what he is doing. Because it occupies such a large part of his life it also dominates his thoughts and conversation. Given the choice he would like an easier career and to spend more time at home. He feels he is missing out on the children growing up. But the family lifestyle has risen to meet his income and he feels trapped. There seems little point in looking for an alternative career. He wants to give his children all of the material things he never had as a child. The children suffer from having little contact with their father. Should we judge this man by the intention behind his behaviour or the consequences of what he does? Should we judge him at all?

In a busy household with many voices filling the air, when there is no time to sit and talk, it is very easy to judge solely on actions and their consequences. And of course, real consequences and actions are the bottom line; the consequences are none the less real for being unintentional. However, if you believe them to be unintentional they may be less painful, because it is usually easier to bear pain if you believe someone did not intend you harm. If we merely judge behaviour, we will miss the intention. Once that occurs, the other party is left feeling misunderstood, punished and pilloried unfairly, and unable to make themselves heard.

We tend to judge ourselves by our intentions and others by their behaviour because the intentions are invisible. It is always worth looking at our intentions and being honest about them. If you buy your partner a present, are you intending to make them feel good or are you looking to gain a favour in return? If it is the latter, then your partner will have some sense of being manipulated, if not immediately then certainly when you seek the favour. Then the next present will be associated not with a good feeling, but with 'What do you want?' Likewise, if we criticize, is our intention to resolve an issue or simply to make the other person feel bad? Are we trying to gain the moral high ground, establish some leverage through guilt or are we trying to bring about a more harmonious relationship? Are we looking to help both of us feel better or are we trying to shape the relationship to suit ourselves?

A step up from ignoring the intention behind behaviour is to assume an intention that suits us. We can read different intentions into any action, it is part of trying to understand other people's behaviour. Rarely do we say, 'I haven't the faintest idea why you did that' – unless as a covert invitation for them to explain themselves.

Some relationships become so bad and both people become so suspicious that everything is presumed to have a double meaning:

'What's for breakfast?' 'Make it yourself!'
'How are you today?' 'I'm fine, why shouldn't I be?'
'Can I help you with that?' 'No, I'm perfectly capable of doing it myself!'
'Are you less busy at work this week?' 'I know, I know, we will go out for that meal soon!'
'I'm just going to visit my mother this afternoon.' 'So you can't even stand being near me now, then?'

We are sure you can supply your own examples.

Mind reading occurs often within arguments:

> 'You left those old shoes there just to annoy me.'
> 'No, I didn't.' (Denying the intention.)
> 'Then who left them there, the Queen?' (Referring to the behaviour.)
> 'I did.' (Accepting responsibility for the behaviour.)
> 'That's what I just said. Just to get at me.' (Re-establishing the validity of the mind read intention.)
> 'No, I didn't.' (Back to the intention.)
> 'You just said you did.' (Reuniting the behaviour with the mind read intention.)

If you think that mind reading is not one of your traits, did you assume we cast the above short scenario as a male talking to a female? If so, which speaker was male and which female? If you mind read that we were stereotyping, look back over that conversation and identify how you knew that.

When someone is trying to read your mind and misinterpreting your intention, rather than get angry at the accusation, simply ask them for the evidence that supports their mind reading. Ask them, 'Exactly how do you know that's what I was trying to do?' And be honest about your real intention.

Sometimes mind reading can be accurate, but then it is not really mind reading, it is noticing and making sense of the body language and non-verbal clues that go with the words. As already noted, women are generally better at this than men are. They are more intuitive because men rely more on words and will interpret what is said far more literally. Women pay more attention to the overall context, the situation and what is *not* said. Woe betide a woman who expects her man to be as intuitive and accurate a mind reader as she is!

Those who mind read habitually believe in their own psychic powers. They also expect others to mind read them accurately. They are often heard saying, 'Well, you should have known' or 'I shouldn't have to tell you that's what I want' or 'Buy me what you think I'd like for Christmas.' This is asking for trouble, especially if it is a woman speaking.

## SUPPORT THROUGH CHANGE

If you are in a relationship your partner has probably come to terms with the way that you are. Even though they may ask you to change, you will both already have adapted. There will be a dynamic between you that works on some level. If you change, even for the better, then the whole balance of the relationship changes. Your partner will be forced to change, even if they do not wish to, in order to respond to the new you.

If one partner tries to bring about change without involving the other partner it can be difficult. First, your change might be resisted and ridiculed by your partner. After all, they can deal with you as you are. If you change then they have to go through the effort of learning a new way of handling you.

Secondly, you might not receive the encouragement, positive feedback and support most of us need to make long and lasting change in our chosen areas.

Thirdly, change may create suspicion. You suggest an evening out and the response you receive is, 'And what have you got to feel guilty about, what are you hiding?'

We all have ideas about our partner. We may feel we know them better than they know themselves. Well, we do not. We do have a different perspective on them than they have on themselves, but no one else can fathom another completely because thoughts and motives, beliefs and values are invisible unless you choose to share them. We only know others from the outside and we only know ourselves from the inside. Neither view is the whole story; we all have a public and a private face. The trouble comes when we attribute inner motives from overt actions. You may be right about the motives, but it is always safest to ask and you usually gain nothing by assuming the worst.

When you are trying to change, even if your partner does not wish to be different, keep them informed of what you are looking to achieve. Let them know the positive impact you expect your change to have on their lives and tell them what support you would appreciate from them. That way you will have more chance of making the changes you want. If you do not have a partner, then enrol a close friend to act as a support.

If you do decide to involve a partner in any changes you wish to make, there are some important rules to share. First, no gloating.

Expressions such as, 'I knew it. If only you'd listened to me in the first place. I told you so but you wouldn't listen. Maybe you'll pay more attention to what I say in the future' will hold back any change you both want to make.

Secondly, let the past stay in the past. You and your partner must allow history to become history. Guilt and blame are the strongest anchors to an unhappy past. They are mirror images of each other. Guilt comes mostly from self-blame and if we want to be without guilt, then we have to give up blaming the other person. So we have to give up feeling justified in what we do and that we were completely in the right. At a deeper level we have to give up the idea that when something goes wrong, automatically someone is to blame. Sometimes things just happen, because the world is not under anyone's control. Sometimes unhappiness is created between the two of you.

Thirdly, let go of past associations as far as possible. When people start to change they are surrounded by past associations that make it harder. For example, if you are looking to stop drinking, the last place you should visit is the pub where you used to drink. Just being there will make you feel thirsty. If you want to make any change easier, go to different places, do different things, wear different clothes, if necessary move to a different house, anything to break the old triggers and give yourself the opportunity to build new, clean associations.

## SPEED OF CHANGE

There are no hard and fast rules about the speed of change. Different methods work for different people in different situations. Some respond best to a slow step-by-step process that allows them to progress in safety. Others like a forceful approach that shocks and thrusts them into a different orbit like a booster rocket on a spacecraft. There was a story in a paper recently of a girl brought up to feel guilty about nudity. Her father had instilled in her a need to keep her body covered. She could not undress unless the lights were out. She could not look on naked people without flushing red with embarrassment. One day she decided she had had enough of this. It was not, she decided, a true reflection of who she was underneath. In an act symbolic of stripping away her conditioned self to expose her true self, she tore off her clothes and ran naked across a rugby field while a match was in progress. She waved to the crowd, picked up the ball and scored a try before being escorted off by police.

I (Robin) experienced sudden change in one area of relationships when I was in my early teens at school. The carpentry teacher, a well-meaning man with a social conscience, organized school funding for me to go on an overseas trip. It was one of many benefits he arranged for me so I did not miss out. I accepted all he did as my due. After all, life had dealt me a bad hand, so I was entitled to some good cards now and again. This made me arrogant. The chips on both shoulders made me swagger.

Then one day I was alone in the schoolroom with this teacher when he lost all control. Frustration flooded from him. He asked, near to tears, why I never said 'Thank you'. All he wanted was a bit of recognition. At first I saw the scene before me as though I was not in it. It was like watching a film in which a distant character was playing my part. Then I connected with myself and saw the man before me. In that instant I realized that other people had feelings. They had needs. And although those feelings and needs were different from mine they were held strongly and were valid. The tears in his eyes showed me that. I wanted to get away. Words of thanks fought to stay inside my mouth. To have expressed gratitude would have been an admittance of the failure of my vision of the world. It would have been a weakness, not manly and, underneath all of that, it would have been an admittance that I was not owed good luck to compensate for my poor luck. That man standing in front of me taught me about personal responsibility. He taught me to empathize. He taught me how to play with the cards I had been dealt. This incident changed my beliefs about the way to respond to misfortune.

I saw him many years later in a hotel lobby. The emotional response I experienced at the time of that learning moment came back to me, triggered by the sight of him. I found the courage to remind him of the confrontation we had been through. I was about to tell him how important it had been for me to learn to say 'Thank you'. I was about to tell him what a difference it had made to my life when he laughed. He nodded knowingly, as if the occasion was as fresh to him as it was to me. I could see the relaxation of his expression, the way his eyes softened as he remembered. He said, 'Yes, I learnt a lot that day. It changed my life. I've never done anything with the expectation of thanks again and it's enabled me to do a lot more and feel better about myself.'


## DRAMATIC CHANGE

There are two sorts of change. One involves gradually adjusting to your chosen partner. This can be fun. You change because you want to. The other type of change is more dramatic. Something is seriously wrong and you have to give or take a lot of ground. In this case, you need to know how you got into that position in order to know what to do for the best.

We say love is blind, and it is hard of hearing too. Not totally blind and deaf, but very selective about what it allows us to see and hear. When we initially meet someone it is common to see only their good points. We are filled with optimism and it seems this new person has brought magic into our lives. Just their presence may promise what we have always looked for and a way of making our lives as complete and wonderful as we deserve. We do not see or hear what might shatter our dreams. We see their good qualities and then add some they do not have to make them perfect.

There is a point in a relationship that occurs after about three months, although it may arrive earlier, where the rose-coloured glasses crack. We start to see people more for what they are. Familiarity breeds understanding. This secondary vision is vitally important because it is the view of the other person that will continue for the rest of your time with them. Whichever combination of your three voices has driven the first three months of the relationship, it is the shift in that balance that will stay with you. The initial sparkle will not return. This is why whirlwind romances often fail in the long-term.

However, some people become obsessed with the magic of these first three months. If they cannot revisit those times with the partner they are with, they will seek new partners. Part of them will want to progress one relationship into something more permanent, whereas another part will keep whispering about the passion and energy of those initial stages.

There are many for whom the genetic voice speaks more loudly than the others do. Many men, especially, are content to have the relationship continue on that level. For many couples this is all they need. Affairs are often based on strong sexual attraction, the element of danger and little else. The film *Last Tango in Paris* told one such story where the man and woman involved had a mutual arrangement not to know each other's name for fear that they might slip away from their single activity focus.

If you want a relationship as opposed to a sexual liaison then you need more than good sex. You need the rest of yourself and you need to know the rest of your partner. Sexual compatibility does not always lead to all-round compatibility and it does not necessarily lead to a long-term relationship, although it is certainly a good start. If you meet someone on holiday and have two weeks of intense sex, do not assume that the relationship will transfer back home. The three 'S's are a potent combination and in the absence of sun and sea, sex is not the same.

Think of three voices like the petals on a flower. If you could rest another flower on top of yours to match perfectly, then the relationship will feel complete and well matched. However, flowers do not always match. When part of you is left unnoticed, unused and unappreciated, it tends to get restless. It seeks recognition, time and utilization. It feels as though it is dying. This is most dangerous if the sexual part is neglected. Couples may mismatch their conditioned voices, in which case one partner may go and spend time with other friends with whom they feel more compatible. A couple may mismatch their intellectual voices, so they will seek out others with whom they can talk about ideas. Neither of these two activities counts as being unfaithful nor are they likely to arouse strong passions in the other partner. But if the sexual voice is mismatched and one partner seeks to satisfy *that* with another, then there is trouble!

Some people stray because just one part of them is left unused. Someone who can bring this one part back to life again will be very attractive because of the days, months or years of frustration built up by neglecting that part. That is why affairs are often brief. Once the dormant part has had its fling, its voice loses volume and the importance of the other parts comes back into play.

Another danger is going too far, too fast, too soon. Some people do not pace the amount they give with the amount that their partner gives or the speed at which they wish to give. Some people think they have to earn love by giving unreservedly from the start. They believe love will resolve all their issues like swallowing a pill and they should, therefore, do everything to ensure it happens. Commitment needs to be paced. There is a danger in giving too much or meeting another's expectations. There needs to be a balance between giving and ensuring you are not vulnerable to misuse.

## CONTROL

Trying to control the other can kill a relationship quicker than anything else can. A good relationship gives people the freedom to be themselves as well as part of the relationship. During the sixties the hippies used to say that if you wanted to hold on to something, then you had to give it away. That was confusing because it sounded like a contradiction. How can you have something that you have given away? It does not make sense until you experience the opposite – holding on to something and finding that you have lost it.

People usually try to control others because they fear losing them or fear that they are not attractive enough in themselves for the other person to stay with them willingly. However, the more you do try to control someone, the more likely you are to lose them. The greater the attempt to control, the greater the corresponding resistance and rebellion. We have known many situations where the use of control has brought about the end of the relationship it was supposed to preserve.

Men tend to use muscle to try to enforce control. Some men reduce a woman's sense of self to the point of helplessness and hopelessness in order for her to feel the need of the man for her own survival. Such women are driven to need the very thing that is making them needy. Such men misinterpret what is said in order to twist its meaning and create guilt. They criticize their partner's appearance and capabilities. They moan how they wish the relationship never started and complain that they are now trapped. They admire other people they see in order to create an unflattering comparison with their partners. Not having the physical presence of the male, and often restricted by concern for children, women may respond with passive resistance. They become unresponsive in bed – the last battlefield – and who can blame them?

Women may try to exert control in a more subtle way. They may use emotional blackmail. They may gain the moral high ground by being easily upset and hurt. They will point out many occasions when the man has been unthinking. This reduces the man's sense of self and creates guilt. The man then feels obliged to compensate. The game of 'If it weren't for you' is a simple way of creating guilt and control for both men and women.

Another control strategy is 'Treat them mean to keep them keen'. Maintaining someone's interest in you by being unpleasant to them, letting them down, being critical of them, feigning lack of interest, flirting with others, being evasive and unattainable and the host of other ploys, is often successful. These strategies work because they throw out a challenge – prove you are man or woman enough to tame me by getting me to love you as much as you appear to love me. This form of enticement demonstrates a need for control often generated by the fear of being controlled. It is connected to primitive forms of enticement and trickery. One of the main difficulties with this strategy is that the meanness tends to escalate until you eventually reach breaking point. How mean you can be to your partner and get away with it becomes a measure of how much they love you.

Some people try to control their partners by shaping them into one of their parents in order to create the love, happiness and safety of childhood. There are many ways to do this and they all involve to some extent becoming more helpless than you really are and expecting the other person to do things for you that you can do yourself, in fact expecting them to 'mummy' or 'daddy' you. The problem is that if they become 'mummy' or daddy', then you will have to become a child again in some way. You will have to become more helpless and because you are actually an adult and not helpless at all, you will feel resentful. You invite them to look after you with one hand while resenting it and pushing them away with the other.

However, if either of you is successful in this quest it is the beginning of the end of your sex life. Your relationship with a parent does not involve sex, so if we turn our partner into a parent, then we must, by definition, not have sex.

There is another danger. The bond between parents and children can be so strong as to dominate the one between you and your partner. Looking after your parents and being true to a parent's values can take precedence over paying attention to your partner. People who put their parents first often deny their partners the right to do the same.

I (Robin) knew a couple where the husband would go to visit his parents every weekend, regardless of what else was happening. His wife could be ill or unhappy and it did not matter – the parents came first. His wife rather liked his parents at the beginning of their marriage, but over the years she came to dislike them intensely through no fault of theirs. The husband used to ask plaintively, 'Why don't you like my parents?' Often this is a signal that the person feels themselves more of a child than an adult, because they put themselves in the position of a child and make it more important than being an adult with their partner. They want to be the most important person in the world to their parents and their partners. But if you give second best to your partner, then that is what you will receive.

If you feel the need to use control, then you risk losing what you evidently want to hold on to. The more control you try and exert, the more you will lose. You lose exactly as much of the other person as you try to control. Go back to your beliefs and values about yourself and relationships and check out what it is that makes you need control. Ask yourself what the payoff is, what are you looking to gain. And find a way other than control to achieve it.

## RESISTANCE

You would think that once you decided to change, it should be easy. It's not. We resist and so do other people. Sometimes the most vocal opponents of the change you want to make are your nearest and dearest.

Honour any resistance you encounter, either in yourself or in your partner. It is the dark side of what was good about the past. We all have our own habits and rituals, we like to make parts of our life as easy and stable as possible so that we can devote our time and energy to more important new projects without having to think about routine matters all the time. This stability comes back to haunt us in the form of resistance. Welcome the resistance. It shows you have done a good job in stabilizing your life up to now. It can be very revealing what parts of our life you take for granted and turn over to habit. Remember habit is what worked in the past. It may not work now or in the future. Make sure that your relationship is not part of your life that you turn over completely to habit, else you will start to take your partner for granted. There is very little difference between 'stable' and 'stale'.

We may be reluctant to change for fear that we might lose something of value. Consider the number of smokers who want to stop, who know the benefits of stopping and the consequences of continuing, and yet who claim to be unable to stop. Certainly, some are addicted chemically. Others are addicted socially. When you delve deeper into their resistance you find that it is not the nicotine that they want but the feeling of alertness, the familiarity of the rituals, the deep breathing or the camaraderie of sharing a smoking break with similar outcasts on the steps of the office in the rain. These are good things, but it is possible to get them without the carcinogens as well.

I (Robin) was working with a man recently who habitually went home late. He did not want to. He knew it upset his wife. He would have preferred to be at home with her but he could not stop himself being late. It was threatening his marriage. We explored the positive by-products of his behaviour by using questions like, 'What would you have to give up if you stopped doing that?' and 'What positive thing does that give you or do for you?' Each time I asked a question this man thought hard. There were many long silences. A summary of his answers were:

'It gives me space and time to think.'
'It gives me a sense of independence.'
'It makes me feel I'm my own man.'
'It makes me feel strong.'
'It makes me feel powerful.'
'It makes me feel nobody can bully me.'
'It makes me feel safe.'

Somehow this man had come to associate, through a number of steps, being late with being safe. Therefore, in order to go home on time he would have had to give up a sense of feeling safe. It was no wonder that his internal voice told him to stay behind when his intelligence was telling him to go home.

Most unwanted behaviour that you have tried to change without success will have powerful positive by-products holding you back. Once you have identified the by-products, you are then in a position to find an alternative way of satisfying that need. For instance, in the case of the man who went home late in order to be safe we found a different way for him to feel safe so that he was free to go home early. All he needed to do was spend more money on shoes to be safe. I am not clear why that action worked, but it did.

If you have a limiting behaviour that you have tried to stop, then make a list of the positive by-products by asking yourself what you gain from such behaviour. What does it produce that you wish to hang on to? For instance, you might find that you are hurtful to your partner in order to prove that you are lovable. How can that be so? Because if they stay with you even though you are hurtful that proves just how lovable you are. Think how much more pleasant life would be if you could express that love in another way.

## Staying the Same...

Why do some people refuse to recognize the need for change in themselves and in their relationship? Of course, many want their relationship to remain just the way it is. It works for them. The fact that it does not work for their partner may be of little or no importance to them. To change may lose them the breadwinner, the servant, a suitable punch-bag on which to vent their frustrations, a compliant sexual partner or someone to moan about.

Others who refuse to change may not want to recognize the mistakes they have made in the past. To change now is to deny what has gone before. Admitting to being wrong is a bitter pill for many to swallow. Spending the rest of their lives fruitlessly trying to prove they are right is often the easiest course for someone whose sense of identity includes infallibility. They do not want to damage their image of perfection. Many do not want to lose face amongst their peers by becoming different. This is especially so with people who are very vocal and opinionated.

Others do not want to change because they are frightened to acknowledge any pain they may have caused to themselves and others. It can be easier to shut out the benefits of change and persist in the same old ways.

If a relationship is to improve, however, both partners may need to change. Without change you stay as you are. If you want a future, let the past go, but not without first learning from it.

## HANDLING DISAGREEMENTS

No relationship exists without disagreements. The best relationships are not those where the partners never disagree, but those where they are able to express and respect their differences. Conflict and difference give life to a relationship, providing they are not so great as to be intolerable. How you handle conflict is of paramount importance to the quality of life and staying together. To ignore a problem does not mean it is not there or that it will not have an effect. Punishing one another in silence is not a solution. When you disagree, do it intelligently – using your intellect to understand the issue and your emotional commitment and energy to solve it.

Whatever the cause or the outcome of disagreements and quarrels, they are always fuelled by not understanding the other person's point of view. There is no completely 'right' perspective here. Men tend to think that with logic on their side they can win any argument, but logic does not win arguments between two people who are emotionally entangled, it only wins arguments when there are no emotions at stake and both people agree that logic is the way to go. Men often think that women are not logical, but this is not true. Women can be very logical when the need arises, but they do not use logic to solve disagreements in close relationships.

Have you ever been in a discussion where you and another person have been in disagreement and then they have said something and suddenly your perspective shifts? The realization comes like a splash of cold water. It happens during arguments between couples quite often. Suddenly one of them is suddenly forced to review their opinion and see the situation from the perspective of the other.

The more we can put ourselves in our partner's shoes and perceive how they understand the world, the better we will be able to communicate with them. With an openness to their point of view we will have a better chance of resolving the issue. It will also make it easier for us to put across our point of view in such a way that they are most likely to understand it.

Have you ever listened to a discussion or argument between two people and just known that the issue will not be resolved? Have you ever watched such a couple and understood their relationship more than they seem to understand it? If you have then it is because that objective viewpoint gave you an understanding that was not available to the couple because they were 'inside' what was taking place. It is this objective viewpoint that makes the roles of cinema director, boxing referee and legal judge such important ones. They have an understanding, because of their objective position, that those involved do not.

To resolve a conflict you need the ability to stand up for your own point of view, a willingness to empathize with and understand the other person and the capacity to be objective. Your perspective is based on your experience, but that does not make it right in a relationship. To empathize with another, you have to make a creative leap into the other person's reality, and the better you know someone, the easier this is. Couples who have been together for a long time often seem to be almost telepathic. This empathy with another is a basic human ability, however we often do not use it at those times when it would be most useful. The ability to appreciate your partner's point of view does not invalidate your own, it is just different. That does not mean it is right either. Then there is the detached perspective that the intellectual voice gives you, from which you can evaluate both points of view and see the similarities and the differences between them. From here you can appreciate your relationship.

Finally, we would add another position to these three basic ones. That is a position that takes into account you as a couple, in a relationship. What is important to you both? How does this disagreement fit with what you both share? What is important to you as a couple and how important is this disagreement in that context?

One way to develop the skill to jump mentally around these three viewpoints is to practise them physically. If we adopt someone's external behaviour we experience their internal state. Matching has shown us that if we copy their body language we receive a sense of the world view that creates that way of acting.

Here's a way you can try this. If your partner has their own chair and tends to sit in that chair in the same posture then, when they are not around, simply sit in that chair in the way that they sit. Give yourself time to settle into the pose, wait until your muscles become familiar with the posture and then become aware of your thoughts and feelings. Sitting like them, become aware of the internal state that triggers that posture. Notice the sort of things you think about, the opinions you hold, what you look at, what your mood is like and your view of the world now that you are sitting in your partner's seat adopting their posture. You may be surprised at what you feel.

If you and your partner are going through this book together you may like to try walking together. Go for a stroll, preferably somewhere secluded to avoid any embarrassment. One of you leads and the other follows, walking in the same way. Again, notice how your senses respond to this experience. Notice what information you take in and how that affects your view of the world and the relationship. Reverse roles and talk about your experiences when you get home.

Here is a good exercise that will help you gain a better understanding of a conflict or disagreement you have, or a situation that you would like to discuss with your partner and which might be contentious or difficult.

---

Sit in a chair and decide how you are going to conduct the conversation, what you hope to achieve, how you will say what you are going to say and what you will say and do if this does not work.

Then stand up, distract yourself, sit in another chair and become, as best you can, your partner. Sit as they would sit. Allow yourself to think as you suspect they would think, making sure that if your internal voice is using the words 'I' or 'me' it is referring to your partner. Decide, as your partner, what you would look to gain from this conversation, how you would structure it and how you would respond to the real you invisibly sitting in the other chair. Having done that, stand up and become your real self again. Then step away from the chairs and take up the objective viewpoint away from both chairs. Now you are outside both you and your partner in that argument. Imagine they are there talking. Watch them talk in your mind's eye. Create a likely conversation from what you have already discovered by sitting in the two chairs. Either internally or out loud, decide what is likely to happen between the invisible people sat on the chairs in front of you. If you refer to them, use their names.

Having gathered this information from these three perspectives, go back and sit down in your chair. Come back to yourself. With the information received from the other two viewpoints, review your approach to the forthcoming conversation. Sometimes you will decide to go ahead as originally planned. That is great and you can now do that with greater confidence. More often you will make adjustments to your approach. Even small variations can have a great influence on what happens.

---

## BALANCING VIEWPOINTS

Sometimes these viewpoints are not as useful as they could be because they are caught up in the limiting beliefs of the conditioned voice. Your first position perspective is not as strong as it might be and the third is not so objective, but gets caught up with conflicting emotions. Here is a way you can refine these viewpoints further. It will also give you a lot of insights into how you view the differences you have with your partner. In this exercise you do not have to move between chairs, you can do it all in your imagination.

---

First think back to a problem or disagreement you have had with your partner.
        Consider it from your own viewpoint.

What do you see?
Where are you looking from?
Are you 'associated', that is, looking out through your own eyes and seeing what you would see from there?

Make sure you are associated, looking out through your own eyes, not seeing yourself from outside.

What is your balance like?
What do you hear?
Whose voices do you hear and where do they come from?
What feelings do you have and where are they in your body?

Imagine the situation again, still looking out of your own eyes. Hear the voices clearly and feel your voice from your throat area. Describe your feelings from your point of view. Feel fully balanced as you do this.

How does this change your view of the situation?
Do you feel more comfortable?

Now go to third position. Imagine seeing both yourself and your partner. Look at the tableau of you and your partner engaged in an argument, disagreement or fight. Notice where you naturally tend to have your viewpoint from this position.

Is it above or below the two of you?
Is it closer to one or the other?

Balance your position by observing the scene from a point equidistant from both of you and from eye level if you are not doing so already. Make sure that both the people in your mental picture are the proper size. Notice if one seems bigger or more solid than the other and change them so they are the same.

Now, from this position, hear your voice and that of your partner coming from where you see them. Hear them through your own ears. This may sound strange, but in our experience many people hear the voices as disembodied and some report that they hear them through the top of their head.

Now, from this position, describe the situation to yourself as you observe it. Let your internal voice come from your throat. When you describe the situation use the pronouns 'he' and 'she'. Save 'I' for yourself as observer.

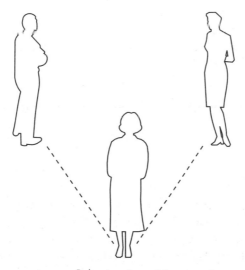

Balancing viewpoints

Now, in this position, if you feel bad or unresourceful, realize that those feelings do not belong to you here. Here you are just observing. Recognize those feeling for what they are and move them to the person to whom they belong. Feel yourself well balanced on both feet.

How do these changes add to your view of the disagreement?

---

This is a very interesting exercise to do because it can show you that how you perceive the situation plays a part in making it difficult for you to resolve it.

I (Joseph) remember doing this with a series of arguments I had with my wife. We just seemed to be going around in circles with the issues and not getting anywhere. I felt under pressure, and when we argued, I did not feel I put my point of view in the best way and I ended up criticizing her ideas instead of putting forward my own.

When I did this last exercise, I found my third position was completely unbalanced. I was leaning towards my side, but what was even more interesting was that I imagined my wife much bigger than me! No wonder I felt it hard to put my point of view. I balanced the positions, I made my third position right in the middle and made us both our natural size. I felt a lot better and the next time the issue came up, I was able to stay calm and put my point of view very well. We still did not agree, but we agreed to amicably disagree. We saw our differences clearly without letting them create a rift between us and I felt very much better about the outcome.

---

When you have balanced these three viewpoints, you can use the next process to explore any difficult situations between you and your partner.

First, what is the problem from your point of view?

What are you trying to achieve that is important to you?

How would you describe what your partner is doing? Choose an adjective that describes how you experience them in that situation, for example, 'pushy', 'argumentative', 'emotional', 'uncaring'.

Now take second position with your partner. Pretend you are them.

How do they see the situation?
What are they trying to achieve that is important to them?
How would they describe what you are doing? Pick an adjective that describes your own behaviour *as experienced by your partner.*

Now switch to third position. Imagine seeing both you and your partner from a detached, calm point of view.

What is your relationship in that situation?
Think of the two adjectives you have thought of – how do they go together?
Do they complement each other – for example, the more one person becomes pushy, the more the other withdraws, or the more one becomes logical, the more the other one becomes emotional?
Are they the same and directly opposed – for example, the pushier one becomes, the pushier the other becomes, or the more rational one becomes, the more rational the other becomes? Whatever the relationship, these two adjectives will feed off each other, one evoking the other in a closed circle.

Then ask yourself, again from third position.

How are you both sustaining the problem by the way you are acting?
If you were to change what you are doing, how would the other person change to deal with your new way of acting?
What would be the benefits to you if that situation changed?
Are those benefits worth you changing the way you are acting?

---

The ability to step outside the situation is the key to solving it. Many arguments are like tennis matches, each partner feels they have to keep returning the ball and each partner usually blames the other partner for serving in the first place. One person's reaction is the other person's trigger. There is a further twist and that is that each expects the other to argue in a particular way and therefore they adopt their own way to counter that, yet looked at from the outside this is exactly what keeps the argument going. Then to cap it all, the situation cannot be discussed because when our warring couple try to discuss it, they fall into the same trap.

To make any change you have to take a metaphorical step outside the situation and see how you are responding to each other. You have to see the relationship, not just the individuals in it. Any solution has to come from a 'we' point of view, for example, 'Whenever *we* talk about this issue, we seem to end up arguing and I don't like that. What can *we* do to help us stop?'

Your partner may reply something like, 'Well, we wouldn't if you weren't so...' At this point do not be drawn. The big temptation is to say something like, 'Well, *I* wouldn't be if *you* weren't so...' All over the world couples have arguments with this same structure and they fill in the blanks in their own way. We take the quality we experience in the relationship and attribute it to the other person. It does not belong to them. It belongs to the relationship. So we say, 'You are bossy' instead of 'I experience you as bossy.' Someone cannot be bossy on their own. These sorts of qualities, good and bad, can only happen *in a relationship*. The same is true for nagging, being overbearing, withdrawing, being angry.

Instead of becoming drawn into your old pattern, you could say, 'OK, how would you prefer me to react?' This is not an admission that you are wrong, just a way of exploring the situation.

---

Now look at the situation of you as a couple.

How does this situation affect your togetherness?
Do you become more or less close as a result?

Look at the effects over time as well.

If this situation were to continue, what might the longer-term impact be?
Are these arguments simply preludes to making up?
How do they affect your relationship over time?
If the situation continued like this would your relationship grow or diminish?

Has this situation built up gradually or did it happen suddenly?
Would it be acceptable to you to be in the same situation as this in six
months?
Three months?
One month?
When in the future will it be essential to change this situation?
Wouldn't it be better to do it sooner rather than later?

---

## Teach Me

Take this exercise as fun. It is best done with a friend, but you can do it
by yourself this first time. It is a simple and fun way to change behaviour
that is standing in the way of the relationships you want. As we go
through the exercise, if you find yourself smiling or saying, 'This is ridicu-
lous,' then stick with it and see what happens.

First, choose a form of behaviour that either hampers the relationship
you are in or restricts you forming the relationships you want. It might be
that you create arguments or you lose your temper easily over small
things. It could be you have mastered the art of shyness or become an
expert at not going to places where suitable companions might be. Make
no mistake, this is a real skill. You do it easily and habitually. You have
invested time and effort into it.

Now imagine yourself in front of a group of people all desperate to learn
how to do the same.

If you do this alone, say the answers out loud if possible. The sound
of your own voice (as opposed to your internal voice) will make a difference.

Here are the questions:

What is it that you're going to teach us? Give us a brief description.
When will we use this behaviour?
     In other words, what is the cue that sets it off?
     How do you know when to start it?
     What habitual set of circumstances has to be present?
With whom will we be using this behaviour?
     Are you discriminating about which people you do it to?
     Does it apply to social classes, or particular people, or only one
     person?

What qualifies a person to be on the receiving end?
And what would disqualify a person from being on the receiving end?
What will we be achieving when we use this behaviour?
What will we get of positive value? There must be something, otherwise why do it?
It is possible that this behaviour achieved something useful a long time ago, perhaps in childhood?
What is the cost of this way of behaving?
What will we lose or risk losing when we learn how to do it?
How often can we expect to succeed in doing it?
What are others likely to think when we behave this way?
Do we need a special belief about other people or ourselves in order to act this way?
How will we know when to stop doing this?
How could we let others know when we were going to stop?
What will life be like when we don't do this anymore?

Mentally go into the future and picture life as it will be without this behaviour. Hear the sounds relating to the new scene, your internal voice, your re-educated conditioned voice and the verbal responses of others involved. See the physical response of others. Notice any feelings associated with the change.

---

This exercise works because it makes you think behind the behaviour. It also enables you to stand back and look at what you did in a detached way. It is no longer part of you, so you do not feel obligated to defend it. A true test of the success of this exercise is that you cannot go back to the old behaviour without feeling uncomfortable. Even better is when you cannot go back to it at all.

Now we need something to replace the behaviour. Nature abhors a vacuum and we cannot give something up without replacing it with something more worthwhile, more in keeping with the self you really want to be. Here is how to find that replacement:

Sit comfortably, be as relaxed as you can, look down on your left side as though you were looking at the floor just beyond your left foot and answer the question: 'What do I want to do differently?' It might be that you want to be better at something or to change some way of behaving that currently does not support you in relationships. Give yourself time to think and for answers to come.

Once you have an answer, ask yourself, 'If I could do that, what would it look like?' As you ponder that question, look up and to the right. See yourself as if you were on a cinema screen assuming the new behaviour. Notice whether there are any physical changes taking place in you as you watch yourself. Does your breathing alter in any way? Notice in the picture how your new behaviour affects other people. Now step into yourself in the picture so that you are no longer objective to the scene but part of it and looking out of your own eyes. As you do this, look down and to the right as though looking at a space just beyond your right foot. Notice how you feel now. Does it feel right and a true representation of you to have this new behaviour?

The eye positions help because they tune your brain to think in different ways. Looking up helps visualization, looking down to the left makes it easy to talk to yourself, while looking down to the right makes it easier to contact your feelings.

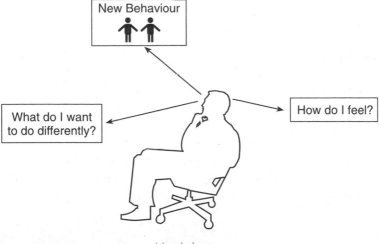

New behaviour

Go through this cycle of three steps at least three times, noticing what happens as you do so. You should find the process becomes smoother, more streamlined. Now create a picture of the future with the new you. Notice the response of others.

Enjoy the difference.

# 7

# Self-Revelation

■ The more of you that you bring to a relationship, the more satisfying it is likely to be. The old saying 'the more you put in, the more you take out' is trite but true. A good relationship means matching the genetic, conditioned and intellectual voices, and underneath the genetic voice, you have to really like someone for a relationship to last. You do not have to like someone to have sex with them. Trust is built up over time; you trust someone when you test them and find they are reliable and not just putting on an agreeable face for your benefit. Some people are fantastic fun to be with and we may have great rapport with them, but we would not choose to spend a lot of time with them.

One way we come to trust someone is by gradually letting more and more of ourselves engage with them in the relationship. We do this by self-revelation – we tell them about ourselves, our thoughts and fears, hopes and dreams, past and future. Self-revelation is one of the most powerful methods of bonding. Self-revelation is telling another person what is true for us and sharing our thoughts with them. As you reveal yourself to another, you discover yourself in the process. The more you know about yourself, the more you can understand yourself and what you want and the more fulfilling the relationship can be. Honesty pushes out doubt and mind reading. Self-revelation says that you are finished with hiding and you trust the other person. Also you trust yourself to be able to reveal yourself. It also enables you both to acknowledge where you agree and where you are different, where you are compatible and where you clash.

I (Joseph) remember walking with my future wife on the hills of Spetse, in the Greek chain of islands. Spetse is very green, not very large, all the holiday areas are concentrated on the coast, and a densely wooded hill rises up in the middle of the island. You can walk from one side of the island to the other in a day very easily. One day we did just that and talked about our lives, past, present and future for the whole time. It was extraordinarily freeing and rather like assembling a jigsaw puzzle. In talking about my life to another person I trusted, I saw its shape more clearly. And in hearing about another person's life, I could understand them better in return.

Self-revelation is always under your control, you can tell as much or as little as you like. We are not saying that you have to tell your partner everything about yourself. That would be foolhardy. We all have thoughts that we do not share with others, actions we want to forget. We are not proposing any sort of psychological soul-baring session. It's more like inviting a friend round for a rich and satisfying meal – you use many different ingredients but you do not have to use the whole contents of your refrigerator. Some things are best left in their containers or should be consigned to the dustbin. Some are well past their sell-by date.

Self-revelation is not about getting rid of problems either. Some people confess their past misdeeds to their partners because then, in their mind, those become their partner's problems, not theirs any more.

We all have our secrets, things that we have done that we feel ashamed of, feelings that we do not like to own, things that do not fit into our identity as we perceive it. Some of these you may tell your partner over time. Some you will not. When you do open out to your partner, and they listen without judging you, a wonderful thing happens. You are accepted. And then you are able to accept yourself more; you become more of yourself and so can give more in turn.

Our conditioned voice implants many beliefs about what is bad and shameful. We often grow up thinking that we have much to be ashamed of, as shame is a standard child-rearing practice in Western European culture. The more you share with others, the more you see that you do not have to feel ashamed. By being accepted by another, we can accept ourselves, and this is very healing. By knowing others, you come to know yourself better, and you realize that you are just two people, each carrying your own baggage from the past, moving into the future on a journey together, helping each other as best you can. Self-revelation is not of course the only way to self-acceptance, but it is a powerful and quick one.

People fall in love over the Internet without ever seeing each other and some even stay together after they meet. People will type in all sorts of ideas and secrets to send to their Internet partners. The computer accepts it all; it does not gasp or break down at your revelations. One reason people fall in love with someone they have never met before is that the honesty, openness and intimacy they are willing to entrust to their computer can create affection with an unseen, otherwise unknown person on the other side of the world.

Self-revelation explains in part how friends can become lovers. People who are not initially attracted to each other on a physical level can grow close as their conversations with each other reveal their true selves over a period of time. With a friendship there is rarely a perceived need to impress, pose or self-project in the way that would attract a member of the opposite sex. What comes out in these conversations is a true description of beliefs and values, and this is how we become attracted.

We ourselves have used self-revelation within this book to show how it works. Hopefully some of the anecdotes will help you know us a little. We have not been completely anonymous, expecting you to examine your relationships in detail while we remain in the shadows.

Self-revelation is very powerful and it can be dangerous. Choose carefully with whom you wish to be open. Trust needs to be earned and takes time to establish, but can be lost in a moment. There is no way of defining how long this should take. You exchange information bit by bit in a way that triggers your internal signals for what is right. Be careful. Honesty and self-revelation are the two most powerful forces in relationships but there are those who will take them and give nothing in return, or even betray your trust.


Here is an exercise that gives you a structure to explore self-revelation using the three voices. This is best shared with a partner, but you can do it alone to uncover some insights about yourself.

When going through this process with a partner, do not rush. You are unlikely to complete the exercise at one sitting. It may be that you break off for a period of consideration and contemplation that can take days. Each step in the process may take your relationship in different directions. It may distance you to begin with and then bring you together. Be prepared at any time to acknowledge that it may not be the right time for you and your partner to be going through this process. Do not feel compelled to cover every question.

This exercise should not be used as a remedial process. If there are outstanding issues between you and your partner, it is best to resolve these first. Self-revelation is a means of getting to know someone fully and building on an already good relationship.

Go through the process step by step, one person at a time. First one partner responds to the questions in their own way, then their partner gives their own self-description. Then share your reactions. Be in the moment when you talk, but be prepared to detach yourself, metaphorically standing outside the conversation and giving your insights in as detached and objective a way as possible. Emotions may arise. Notice them, let them fade and then decide if you want to continue. The sequence and the questions are only suggestions, but we think they give a good structure to the process of self-revelation. You may leave out many questions and put in some of your own.

You may find the genetic voice and the conditioned voice merging and clouding as you go through this process. This is OK. Many people are walking around believing themselves to be genetically programmed machines with no control or choice. An awareness of the blurred overlap between the genetic voice and the conditioned voice is useful in showing that nothing we do in relationships is completely instinctive and completely outside our control.

We will cover our three voices starting with the genetic and moving through the conditioned to the intellectual. We use this sequence because we are born with our genes, we take on board our conditioning and we develop our intellectual, objective and common sense voice through our experience of life.

Not to complete this exercise is not a sign of failure or a poor relationship. Neither is deciding not to start the process. Be aware of your boundaries and those of your partner and do not go beyond them.

First some guidelines for this process:

---

If you are doing this with a partner, decide who is comfortable going first.
If it is you, give your point of view.
Then listen to what your partner has to say if they want to respond before going through the exercise themselves.
No criticism is allowed from either side while the other is speaking.
All comments should be self-referenced and owned: 'I think...' or

'I feel...' or 'I believe...' No judgements. No arguments. You are saying what is true for you and hearing what is true for your partner.

---

## The Genetic Voice
### Physical Attraction

The first question is simple enough:

What physical attributes turn you on?

Each partner describes what physical appearance of the opposite sex attract them or turn them on – curves, muscles, eyes and hair.

It might be that a certain colouring appeals to you. It might be the height or build of a person that attracts you. It could be big bosoms or small bottoms – be honest.

While you do this, you may become aware of how the other two voices interact. Do you feel that owning up to liking large bottoms is not really acceptable? And it doesn't make sense, but who cares? Are you triggered initially by genetic drives and then your conditioning and intellect step in to provide a rounded view of how the relationship is likely to go with someone with those physical qualities? Or does your genetic voice run the show?

Have all your partners had those attributes that you have spoken of? Do the other voices have to wait their turn until after sex? Do you believe that this voice is all there is?

If you find that after physical satisfaction there is little to hold you to the other person, it is likely that the only way in which you are compatible is physical. There is nothing wrong with that as long as it suits both of you. Difficulties will arise, however, when age and gravity take their toll of the physical qualities that draw you.

Stay calm, whatever is said, even if your partner talks about features that you feel you do not have. This is especially so when one of you has changed their appearance or put on weight. The purpose of this section is to understand each other better and to see if there are ways in which you could be even more attracted to each other. It is not to find a stick with which to beat the other. Physical attractiveness is important, but it is only one part of a relationship. And of course beauty is in the eye of the beholder. If your partner describes features you feel you do not have, it is quite possible they see them in you even if you do not.

You may find your partner matches your physical criteria perfectly, in which case your genetic voice is strong and you pay attention to it. This is great as long as you are compatible in other ways. If you think your partner hardly matches any of the features, then this tells you that the genetic voice is weak and the other voices are stronger.

---

Throughout a relationship our appearance changes. We look in the mirror every day and the small changes accumulate, never obvious from day to day, but a shock when we compare ourselves with a photograph from years ago. We look in the mirror and may wonder, 'What on Earth happened here?!' When did it happen? We never noticed, yet slowly but surely the years take their toll on those things the genetic voice loves so much.

The problem is that the genetic voice never gets updated. Whatever our age, the genetic voice still favours the youthful curves, the good complexion, the shining hair, all those signs of health that evolution makes us attracted to despite ourselves. This is usually more of a problem for men. In men the genetic voice is stronger. Generally speaking, men pay more attention to physical appearance than women and are immediately attracted by physical beauty. We age, but our genetic voice gives us the same message – go after youth, go after beauty, go after health. And so we see men chasing women who are young enough to be their daughters, while their men friends laugh, or feel envious depending on what happens. They are ambivalent – they want him to succeed, because it gives them hope for themselves, but they want him to fail, else they would feel envious. As we write this, there are a number of films showing where the leading man is very much older than the leading lady, but they fall in love. Evolutionary male wish-fulfilment. These relationships can work, but not very often. The couple must have something else in common. One of the challenges of age is to educate the genetic voice, so while we can appreciate physical beauty it does not have the tremendous magnetism it had in our youth.

This exercise can also provide the motivation to be healthier, because gradually, without knowing, we can allow the way we look to slip. When I (Robin) went through this exercise with my wife, it gave me the final motivation to exercise and diet.

## Sexual Preferences

During this time be honest about the amount of sexual activity that you desire, what form that activity takes, the amount of foreplay that best stimulates you and the sort of activities that most appeal to you. This is when the conditioned voice will make its presence felt. Sex is biological, but our upbringing and social conditioning influence what sort of sex we like and whether we find that acceptable.

There are some people who believe they have extremely high sex drives with a strong need for frequent activity that is totally part of their physical being. For some of them this is true; others seem to be motivated by self-doubt and low self-esteem – high sexual activity is their means of bolstering their sense of self. When sexual activity is used to raise self-esteem, life can become dominated by sex, sex becomes compulsive and compulsions are defences against threat. The way to tell is to notice what reaction you have when you are denied your usual form and frequency of sexual activity. If you feel frustrated, then this is simple, but if you feel anxious, then there is something else going on. Anxiety is the signal that you feel under threat and it may be your self-esteem that is threatened.

In this exploration you may find your partner desires sexual behaviour that you do not agree with. What they desire may be uncomfortable, dangerous or illegal. They might also want to do things that turn you off. This is difficult territory. However, if your relationship is strong, you may be able to accommodate each other through fantasies. Do not force yourself to do anything you strongly disagree with or feel uncomfortable about and do not expect your partner to either.

## How You Attract Prospective Partners

This section you can do alone.

How do you typically try to attract partners?

The way you use to attract partners is often the way you use to keep them too. We keep doing what works. For instance, if a man attracts women through physique, power, position or dominance, these are the ways in which he is likely to hold that relationship together. A woman may find these initial qualities instantly attractive but logically may choose not to spend too much time living with them. Likewise, a man may find a woman who oozes sexuality instantly captivating, but this may not necessarily be what he would be looking for in a long-term partner, presupposing that a long-term relationship is what he wants.

One way men attract women is by offering them protection. The need for men to be the protector and women to be the protected still lives on with many couples. Some men like their women to be dependent upon them. Some women like to be looked after. Some men are intimidated by women who are assertive or who show they are self-sufficient. Some women hate men who cannot stand up for themselves. Some of this is hard-wired, although most of it must surely be conditioned behaviour perpetuated and passed on through the generations.

It is worth talking with your partner about your need to be protected or to protect. It can have an impact on the size of the partner we choose, if nothing else. The attraction of small women to big men is quite common. It can also influence how in control a woman wants her man to be and how submissive a man wants his woman to be. Protection and control can grow into possession and dominance if you are not careful – what was once comforting can become smothering and limiting.

## The Conditioned Voice

### Attitude to the Opposite Sex

What do you think of the opposite sex?
What attitudes and expectations do you have of them?

Here are some questions to help you explore this area:

What tasks do you take care of in the relationship?
Are you happy to do those tasks?
Do you think you should be doing those tasks?
Are there any tasks that you feel you should be doing that you are not doing and this feels wrong to you?
What do you think women are good at?
What do you think men are good at?

Women have been traditionally the weaker sex in muscular strength and up until quite recently in power and influence too. When men or women have positions of power they strive to keep them. Do you not think that democratic government would work more effectively and more fairly if the members that made up the government were a representation of the sexes, ages, racial and religious groups that they governed?

You may find your attitudes coming out in your work. I (Robin) have no difficulty in working for or employing women. However, as a four-year-old I would gather my gang around me and make fun of the girls in the class. I knew at that age that boys and girls were suited to different activities. My mother's influence on me reinforced this idea. She kept me away from domestic duties and piled them upon my sister. I remember employing men and women to do the same job and knowing it was right to pay them different salaries. Then I started to use my intellect. I noticed that in many ways, women were more capable of getting the work done. I saw how easily male-dominated governments reverted to conflict to resolve confrontations. Male dominance usually leads to a lack of balance, a lack of compassion and less concern for the individual. It tends to be a muscular capitalism where the weak go to the wall with the implicit idea that somehow they deserve to because at some level they are to blame for their weakness. These attitudes can also be found at a smaller level in the workplace.

If you are a man it is useful to know what deep-rooted instincts you hold regarding the roles of men and women. You may then make a choice of overriding or controlling those instincts. If you are a woman it would be useful to know what you expect of men and what your experience leads you to expect.

Our attitudes to the opposite sex are the result of a complex mixture of evolutionary differences, social norms, historical factors and the family environment, and so shade into the socially conditioned aspect of relationships.

Very often we learn about a partner's background and upbringing by meeting their parents and siblings, and visiting their homes. However, it is useful to talk through what childhood has been like, what was good and what was bad. If you have not met your partner's parents in person it is useful to find out more about your partner's ideas about their parents' beliefs and values.

It is also good to talk about how other people's beliefs and values have affected you. Years ago I (Robin) suffered silent ridicule when discussing my future with the careers master at school. Because I was athletic and muscular, he decided I should become a policeman. I said, after much hesitation, that I wanted to do something more creative. He laughed at that and looked at my file. Having noticed that I was good at art and technical drawing he ignored my protestations and arranged a job interview for me in an engineering drawing office. I got the job. I trained to draw construction plans for drainage systems. It was like being in a Kafka novel where I was the only sane person amongst a group who were enthralled by straight lines, water flows and waste disposal. In no time at all I began to think that it must be me who was mad.

Understanding your partner's natural aptitudes makes a world of difference to the way you support them in having the life they want. What they do for the benefit of the relationship may not be an expression of their true selves, so you will appreciate them more. If life dictates that one or both of you have to do things that you do not like and do not suit you, it is important that the other partner recognizes the sacrifice. It is also important that you both work towards creating a balance between what you do and what you want to do.

## Expectations of the Partner's Role in Life, at Work and in the Home

You may be tempted at this point to express a logical, common sense point of view. You will have the opportunity for that later. This is your chance to say what your *conditioning* leads you to believe is the role of your partner and what they should be good at doing.

I (Robin) remember early in our marriage my wife tried to coerce me into decorating. Her father had been a keen and expert decorator. I hate it. I get bored after four minutes of holding a paintbrush and would rather go to prison than earn my living as a paperhanger. Anyway, to make the peace and to please my wife, I agreed to decorate our kitchen. It was afterwards that a friend adept at do-it-yourself pointed out that while papering behind the cooker's electrical socket, I had come perilously close to death by electrocution. Since then my wife and I have both agreed, logically, that when some DIY work needs to be done, we get someone in to do it who is properly trained. Likewise, having had a house proud mother who loved nothing more than to cook, I still find it hard to apply my intellect and not feel puzzled that my wife does not gain the same satisfaction from cooking.

Being aware of what we have been conditioned to expect of our partners, both at work and domestically, is the first step to deciding realistically what you are both good at and what is best for both of you.

## The Parental Home

Here is where you can discuss how your partner would have fitted in with your childhood home. You may already know how they fit in with your family now. Describe the ways you feel they would match or mismatch with your home life as a child. This section will reveal if you have been attracted to someone similar to you or whether you are looking for someone to compensate for what you may be lacking.

## Sexual Preferences and Inhibitions

The conditioned voice sometimes shouts louder than the genetic voice. In relationships our instincts can tell us one thing and our conditioned voice stops our bodies doing it. In many respects this is good, as there are physical and emotional dangers in having no controls. However, difficulties occur when our intellectual voice says that it is now safe to go with our instincts yet our conditioned voice does not give way. If the conditioning has come from your parents it is hard to have the sex you want with your parents metaphorically looking over your shoulder.

It is important at this stage to discuss and reveal the amount and type of sexual activity that your conditioned voice permits you to have. It can be frustrating when partners feel they have genetic sexual compatibility but conditioning gets in the way. An open discussion here can identify which beliefs and values around sexual activity may be limiting you both.

---

## Talking through the Levels

Here you can talk about your sense of self.

How do you perceive yourself?
What sort of person are you? Tell your partner just in one sentence, starting with, 'I am...' For example:

> 'I am a caring person...'
> 'I am someone who gets what they want...'
> 'I am a generous person...'

Tell your partner something that happened in your life that is absolutely typical of you. If you could pick out one or two things that happened to you that really show the sort of person you are, what would they be? Tell them one or two defining moments in your life.

> What happened that really had a profound effect on you?
> Was it a person? A misfortune? A tragedy? A wonderful experience?
> What life experiences have had the most effect on making you the person you are now?

Now tell your partner about what is important to you.
What do you value in a relationship?
You may have already done some work with beliefs and values
*(see pp.58–73)*. Now would be the time to share those with your
partner.

---

## The Intellectual Voice

Here is where you can talk about what you have observed to be true
and important in relationships as opposed to what you wish were
true and important, or what you have been brought up to believe to
be true and important.

For example, you might want to achieve certain objectives before
you make a commitment to a relationship. Even though money might not
seem important to you, you may have noticed that financial difficulties
make life difficult and therefore you would want to be financially secure
before considering a commitment.

Here you can also talk about what expectations you both have in
life. This is important to share because if your ambitions are very different,
it can drive a wedge between you. This is where you can talk about what
you want individually and what you want together.

Be realistic. This does not mean not being ambitious. There is nothing inherently wrong with goals, expectations and dreams as long as
they bring happiness. The dreams and drives that seem to bring unhappiness are those that are unrealistic from the start.

---

I (Robin) once attended a seminar where the thrust of the message was
that anybody could have absolutely anything in life as long as they
wanted it enough. It was a good positive message, but I felt it was making promises it could not deliver. My concern was for the many people
who might leave the seminar full of enthusiasm only to experience a
double dose of personal failure if they did not get what they had been
told they should be able to get.

When the presenter forcefully stated that we could all achieve
absolutely anything for the twentieth time, I asked if he could design a
puzzle that he was not capable of solving. He looked blank and his eyes
rolled. 'Why did you ask me that?' he said.

'Because you said anybody could do anything,' I replied.

'Well, it all depends...' he started.

'Thank you,' I said and sat down. 'That was what I wanted to know.'

## WHAT IS LOVE?

Industries are built on defining love. Valentine's Day cards use millions of words in an attempt to transport its meaning from one person to another. But the love is not in the card, but in the thought of sending a card.

There was once a series of cartoons that seemed to be never ending where each day a new definition was added to the words 'Love is...' The book and film *Love Story* climaxed on the declaration that love is 'never having to say you're sorry'. We feel that anyone who took this definition literally would be in for a nasty surprise. During our research we asked many of our friends for a definition of love. Even those who answered took an age to do so. Many just looked blank or choked on their coffee. Some became uncomfortable. It is an awkward question, and a little unfair, because love is not one thing. It is something you experience, not something you define. There is no right answer, this is not an examination question, and yet in a way it is. Because your definition of love, while it may not tell us much about that most complex of human emotions, will tell you a lot about yourself. You might have hoped for a succinct and telling phrase that would summarize the meaning of love forever. The phrase has evaded us.

What makes love difficult to define? After all, we could all be fairly accurate about hatred or dislike or disgust. If love were easy to define there would be far fewer songs in the world. Great poets might never have written. Many movies would never have been made. One reason why it is so hard to define is that we ask the word to do too much. We love our mate in life, our children, parents, friends, apple pie and our favourite music. We stretch the word until it becomes commonplace and transparent.

Love means different things to different people at different times and at different stages of a relationship. At the beginning of a relationship when there is discovery, risk, promise and excitement, love can be an overwhelming experience that puts you in touch with emotions that normally lie dormant.

Love is supposed to solve all your problems, but nothing will do that for any length of time. Love has many levels and words can never do it justice. The nearest we can come is with a metaphor – we do not say what love is, but we say love is like...

What metaphor do you have for love? Love is like...

Easier to say what love does. We feel wonderful. Someone else is more important to us than ourselves. We are drawn to them, we want to be with them, they have the answer, we feel as if the myth is true and every person is a perfect couple that has been separated and life's task is to find that partner and be reunited. And love tells us we have found them.


There are two states that will stop love. The first is perfectionism. The perfect partner is an illusion. There is not one person, one perfect special person who will make all your dreams come true. And you do not have to be perfect to be worthy of love. Despite the compelling myth, you are not half a person looking for someone who has a half person to spare who will make you whole. You are a complete person looking for another complete person looking to make a complete couple. In a good relationship, you both become more of the people you are, and your relationship enhances you, not diminishes you. And love does not conquer everything. In fact it can get in the way of many things because it takes up so much time.

The second enemy of love is indifference. Hate is not the opposite to love; indifference is. At least when you hate someone you care. What they do affects you. When you are indifferent you do not care.

Love at first sight is not some magic spell that sparkles when two people first look at each other. It is mutual recognition of familiarity and seeing someone who comes close to the image of the ideal partner that you have in your head. You may not even know when true love 'strikes'. It can be there for years before you see it.

Love may be a combination of physical attraction, the desire for intimacy, a passion that is generated by proximity, a willingness for commitment, compatibility in our three voices, friendship, a shared view of the world, care and concern for each other, deep understanding and many other emotions and needs that are individual to the person or the relationship.

Love involves commitment. Commitment means valuing your partner and your relationship very highly. It means staying with them and caring for them not only when you want to – that is easy – but when you do not want to, because you know that over time that is the right thing to do. So commitment involves having a longer timeline, being able to see past the satisfaction of the moment, being able to put aside present personal satisfaction for that of another person because that relationship is more important. Love without commitment is feeling divorced from continuity. Can you have love without commitment? Probably not. People are not frightened of commitment as such. Many are, however, frightened of committing to the wrong person. If they are unwilling to commit, there is little chance of love.

Love makes you capable of extraordinary things, you find yourself saying things and doing things that you had never considered possible. What you do and what you are capable of show the quality of your love. Actions are what count. They define love. Love is not something that strikes magically and then you become a good person and the relationship becomes easy. When the first flush of love fades, you have to work to keep it alive.

What is the most memorable pleasant experience of your life? What do you recall really clearly? What moment would you love to recapture? For many people it is their first kiss and research presented to the American Psychological Society in 1999 backed this up. We do not need a psychological society to tell us the first kiss is a wonderful experience, but it was surprising that it came out as one of life's most pleasant memorable events, above marriage and the first experience of sexual intercourse. Couples recalled nearly all the details surrounding the first kiss, from the colour of their clothes, to the exact place and the first words they said afterwards. With your first kiss, the world opens out. It is the gateway from childhood to being an adult and a sexual identity. And it is intensely pleasurable. As you think back to that kiss now, how it was, what it felt like, what you saw and what you heard, wouldn't it be wonderful if your relationship now could have that magic in them, that pleasure, that promise, that total newness? We hope they can.

# About the Authors

**Robin Prior** is a management consultant, business trainer and author with many years' experience in Neuro-Linguistic Programming (NLP). He is an executive coach, is particularly interested in humour and writes scripts for television. He helps others and himself to achieve balance between their professional life and personal life.

He is the author (with Joseph O'Connor) of *Successful Selling with NLP*.

**Joseph O'Connor** is a leading author, trainer and consultant in the fields of systems thinking, personal development and leadership. He is a certified trainer in NLP.

Joseph gives training on NLP, systems thinking and leadership in Europe, Asia and North and South America. Corporate clients include: UNIDO, BA, BT, Hewlett-Packard and ICI.

His bestselling book *Introducing NLP*, written with John Seymour, is established as the basic introductory text in Neuro-Linguistic Programming and has been translated into 14 languages. Joseph's other books have also been published in several languages.

Joseph lives with his wife and two daughters in London.

## OTHER BOOKS

*Not Pulling Strings*
*Extraordinary Solutions to Everyday Problems*
*Leading with NLP*
*Introducing Neuro-Linguistic Programming* (with John Seymour)
*Training with NLP* (with John Seymour)
*Successful Selling with NLP* (with Robin Prior)
*Principles of NLP* (with Ian McDermott)
*Practical NLP for Managers* (with Ian McDermott)
*NLP and Health* (with Ian McDermott)
*The Art of Systems Thinking* (with Ian McDermott)

## AUDIOTAPES

*Leading with NLP*
*An Introduction to NLP* (with Ian McDermott)
*NLP Health and Well-being* (with Ian McDermott)

If you are interested in finding out more about NLP training as well as
other ways of applying the ideas in this book to relationships, contact:

Lambent Training
4 Coombe Gardens
New Malden
Surrey
KT3 4AA
UK

Telephone and fax: 020 8715 2560
E-mail: lambent@well.com
Website: www.lambent.com

# Index